Management for Professionals

More information about this series at http://www.springer.com/series/10101

Gunther Friedl • Andreas Biagosch
Editors

Case Studies in Strategic Management

How Executive Input Enables Students' Development

Springer

Editors
Gunther Friedl
TUM School of Management
Technical University of Munich
Munich, Germany

Andreas Biagosch
TUM School of Management
Technical University of Munich
Munich, Germany

ISSN 2192-8096 ISSN 2192-810X (electronic)
Management for Professionals
ISBN 978-3-030-07057-1 ISBN 978-3-319-95555-1 (eBook)
https://doi.org/10.1007/978-3-319-95555-1

Softcover re-print of the Hardcover 1st edition 2019

This Springer imprint is published by the registered company Springer Nature Switzerland AG
The registered company address is: Gewerbestrasse 11, 6330 Cham, Switzerland

Preface

Preparing the next generation of business leaders is a core challenge in achieving educational excellence. To this end, we have developed a series of advanced case study teaching seminars with a unique approach at *TUM School of Management.*

Advances in management accounting are happening at lightning speed. New and innovative ideas and insights occur almost daily. Reflecting these innovations in effective education increasingly requires educators to bridge theory and practice at university level. While there is general agreement on this point, implementation is less easy. The use of case studies at famous universities such as the Harvard Business School and other top-ranking institutions has gone a long way toward addressing this need and is already well established. In now famous case studies, student teams analyze and write up real-world cases in hindsight. The outcomes are of course known since the cases selected have happened. Student teams have to develop the case logic building from the situation and its complications and define the critical core issue that finally led to the known outcome. This type of case study remains popular because it is a good way to apply methods, concepts, and specific analyses to real business situations. Students review how certain analyses may have led to particular decisions. They can draw on published comments from involved business leaders on their thinking, attitude, and judgment at a certain time in the case and thus can gain insight into the reality of business practice. We are confident that the majority of our readers have experience and insight gained from conducting their own case studies.

Real business situations and decisions, however, are subject to unknown future influences and indeterminate outcomes. Business leaders are constrained to deal with unresolved cases and to anticipate likely outcomes based on appropriate analyses and insights and, indeed, judgment based on their individual experience. The latter is often as important as analytical logic. It is this uncertain situation in typical business reality that we aim to teach and prepare students for. *The TUM advanced case study seminar* focuses on cases with speculative solutions such as future initial public offerings (IPOs), hypothetical mergers, or expected start-up developments and possible exits—all with no known or previously published outcome.

We believe that applying their learning in making recommendations for real situations is of great value to students, if done effectively. This will happen if experienced practitioners, executives, and/or experts are involved and give specific feedback on the case logic and recommendations. There are well-known approaches and techniques to solving cases and special analyses for certain cases, e.g., an enterprise evaluation or an equity storyline for an IPO. We call these elements "necessary" for any IPO, but a recommendation for an IPO only becomes "sufficient" if an insider's perspective is added. Not that this insider is automatically right, but their input lends a case recommendation practical value. If you can argue that the public owner is a better owner for the company's future than the current owner, you have a convincing case.

The purpose of this book is to convince other faculties engaged in case study teaching to steer their approach in the same or similar direction, i.e., allow student teams to select an actual case of their choice and help them to approach and solve it in order to come as close as possible to real executive thinking. In order to do this successfully, two faculty talents need to come together. Firstly, the teaching of concepts and analyses that are crucial for analyzing and assessing cases such as company evaluations or IPO situations. Secondly, to draw on the experience of real business leaders in terms of how he or she would approach the case selected. Feedback is here delivered and organized by an experienced senior consultant with the appropriate network to engage the right executives and/or experts on different cases.

Both these elements have proved invaluable in the *TUM School of Management* case study seminars. These are run by Gunther Friedl, Dean of the *TUM School of Management*, with a team of engaged postgraduates directly supporting student teams on their specific case studies. Providing practical experience and bringing together the right executives and experts is Dr. Andreas Biagosch, who served as a McKinsey consultant for almost three decades encompassing many different industries and their leading companies.

With the hope that the purpose of this advanced seminar and this book is roughly clear, we would like to involve you the reader in our approach. Since we teach using case studies, we explain our purpose in a case study format. The following chapter presents the case and explains the path to the approach in detail, elaborating on the experience gathered from 90 cases. It also contains students' reactions and feedback to this format, which has so far been extremely encouraging and convinced us of the value of continuing with this approach.

Having read the case study of the seminar, the reader may wish to know what kind of executives and/or experts helped with their feedback and judgment to make this educational experience one of the best—if not *the* best—of the students' education. The list contains all those leaders involved in the seminar who were crucial to its success. Without them, the students' work could not have been so fabulously reviewed. These executives and experts provide a unique window on what students will experience later in their business life. Our heartfelt thanks are due to all the participants in the name of all seminar students and the faculty.

Two cases from this seminar won an international case writing competition, and we congratulate the student teams on their success. We also felt it would be appropriate to publish these two cases in this book for interested readers. The "*unu* scooters development" is still going well and only time will tell to what extent the case study team's predictions are realized and whether their recommendations prove helpful. The case study on "*UBS* acquires *Commerzbank*" was worked out in the summer of 2016. After the student team started this case study, the then CEO of *Commerzbank*, Martin Blessing, left and joined the board of the *UBS*. You can imagine the speculation this caused in our seminar. There is as yet no acquisition of *Commerzbank*, despite new speculation at the end of 2017. It remains exciting for all who were involved in the case—great proof of the excitement actual case studies can generate. We hope also for you as the reader.

Munich, Germany
May 2018

G. Friedl
A. Biagosch

Acknowledgements

This special seminar format can only come to fruition and provide output when students voluntarily subscribe to the enterprise. Every semester, 30 students are selected from a larger group. These students work hard to define and work through their case. The authors are grateful for the students' creative case ideas and their relevant contributions and excellent write-ups. The students also have to present their ideas to executives and experts, thus taking the courage to recommend their findings to true insiders. Their efforts almost always yield very good grades. Perhaps more importantly, the students gain the respect of the executives and experts. We therefore extend our particular thanks to the students for being such effective "ambassadors" of the TUM.

A big thank you goes to all the invited executives and experts. The discussion with these managers is the highlight for all the participating students and for the faculty. We dedicate Chap. 3 to the great contributions of outstanding individuals who attend the seminar and make the time and effort to improve the students' case recommendations and support their argumentation. Many of the managers come twice or even more often and often have to travel far. They should know that the students will remember their session with them for many years to come and value this as an outstanding event in their education. It is important to mention here that the faculty also benefits tremendously from the experts' comments and appreciates the interaction with them enormously.

The well-founded case logic and first-class presentations would not come together without the intensive support of the tutors at the *TUM School of Management*. They give a lot of guidance during the case work, help in Q&A, and often do dry runs to prepare students to deliver convincing presentations. They also offer considerable support in producing the written case studies. They finally recommend an evaluation of the student team output that is discussed and calibrated with the senior faculty for a final grade. All Ph.D. students who supported as tutors in different semesters between 2013 and 2017 received good to outstanding feedback from students and are much appreciated by the authors.

Maximilian Blaschke	David Matthäus
Gerald Broneske	Iris Pfeiffer
Gerke Gersema	Christopher Scheubel
Gunther Glenk	Peter Schäfer
Cornelia Hojer	Friedrich Walcher
Friedrich Kley	Alexandra Zehe
Verena Limbrunner	

Special thanks go to the two student teams whose cases won in the EFMD case writing competition. They also earned our respect for having participated and won in this demanding international competition. We are glad that they allowed us to publish the *unu* scooter case by Franziska Beck, Michael Krauß, and Frieder Weidenbach and the *UBS–Commerzbank* banking case by Philipp Deisler, Michael Eisenlauer, and Fahrudin Abazi in this book.

A good book must be typed, figures drawn, composition optimized, and text edited. For these key contributions, great thanks are due to Martina Hechl, Friedrich Walcher, Yanis Gamarra, and editor Karl Detering with his team. They contributed significantly to the current appearance of the book.

Last but not least, we are grateful for positive interaction with Springer Publishers and in particular to Rocio Torregrosa. It was a constructive and effective collaboration.

Contents

About the Authors

Gunther Friedl has been dean of the TUM School of Management at Technical University of Munich since 2010. He joined TUM as a full professor of management accounting in 2007. Gunther Friedl holds both a Diploma (M.Sc.) in business administration from the University of Munich and a Diploma (M.Sc.) in physics from Technical University of Munich. He received his Dr. (Ph.D.) and habilitation in business administration from the University of Munich. Before joining the Technical University of Munich, Gunther Friedl has been full professor at the University of Mainz. He has been a visiting scholar at Stanford University and a guest professor at Warsaw School of Economics. Gunther Friedl is author and coauthor of several textbooks and monographs on management accounting. He has won several awards, including the "Best Teaching Award" at TUM School of Management over successive years. He shares a passion for bridging science and practical management experience with his coauthor.

Andreas Biagosch was educated at TUM where he studied mechanical engineering and business administration. From 1984 to 2012, he served as consultant at McKinsey & Co.—the last 12 years also as an elected member of its worldwide board, the shareholders council. He did his client work for leading companies in the global automotive, aerospace, and high-tech industries. In recent years, he has served as non-executive board member at global companies which are mostly family-owned. Besides this, he is passionate about passing on his practical management experience from hundreds of important client projects to students via case studies of current or future topics.

List of Abbreviations

CEO	Chief Executive Officer
CFO	Chief Financial Officer
CRISPR-CAS9	Clustered Regularly Interspaced Short Palindromic Repeats with protein-9 nuclease (Cas 9), a method for Focused Genome Editing
EFMD	European Foundation for Management Development
FCA	Fiat Chrysler Association
IPO	Initial Public Offering
IT	Information Technology
M&A	Merger and Acquisition
MVV	Munich Municipal Transportation
NGO	Non-governmental Organization
Q&A	Questions and Answers
SWOT	Strengths, Weaknesses, Opportunities, Threats
TUM	Technical University of Munich

List of Figures

Case: UBS—Acquisition of Commerzbank AG as a Possible Growth Strategy

Case: The Renewed Case Seminar

Andreas Biagosch

On a summer afternoon in Munich in 2013, Gunther Friedl, Dean of *TUM School of Management* and Andreas Biagosch, recently retired from *McKinsey & Company* after 28 years, were exchanging ideas on how to create the most inspiring business seminar. Their goal was to create an outstanding learning experience for business students. Thus the case study seminar at the Technical University of Munich School of Management was born. We brainstormed several initial ideas.

1 Brainstorming

Today's and tomorrow's cases The cases studied should not be outdated. Traditional case studies argue in hindsight and propose best solutions to known issues. This new case seminar should consider current issues of major relevance or even ideas for possible future cases. Such cases are of course open-ended because the best solution is as yet unknown. Students should be looking for an answer to tomorrow's cases. The case study topics build on emerging technologies or new businesses evolving from innovations or digitalization. Rather than analyzing what has been written and published about cases in hindsight, they need to be developing and creating smart solutions with current relevance for business leaders. The cases should create excitement for the student teams working on them as well as for the participating executives, the other students in the seminar and the teaching staff. Ideally, the cases would be of interest to a broader public, including the readers of these pages.

A. Biagosch (✉)
Technical University of Munich, Munich, Germany
e-mail: biagosch@impacting1.com

G. Friedl, A. Biagosch (eds.), *Case Studies in Strategic Management*,
Management for Professionals, https://doi.org/10.1007/978-3-319-95555-1_1

Case examples were anticipated. Upcoming IPOs or mergers in consolidating industries were imagined. In 2013, internet companies like *Zalando* were expected to make an IPO, and mergers between *Lufthansa* and (at that time thriving) *Turkish Airlines* could be imagined, but were not publicly discussed. Similarly, the application of state-of-the-art technologies in startups as well as in both new and in mature industries, such as the supercharger infrastructure at *Tesla*, were potential cases. Obviously the narrowness of the *TUM* with its leading technical expertise and closely located top companies like *BMW* with their new *iSeries* came to mind. Likewise *Siemens* acquiring wind power companies or *Airbus* selling its defense business. Beyond all the commercially oriented cases we also considered NGOs and not-for-profit organizations, e.g. *TUM*, *Bavarian Opera* or the *Deutsche Museum* to name a few.

Self-selection preferred The excitement of creating cases of current interest was something we wanted to give to students. This would not only inject new life into case study teaching, but allow students to select their own topics in pursuit of their individual interests. Students would be supported in creating and generating exciting cases. Their choices could be triggered using examples but they should not be forced to pick any particular one. Support of their selection would involve a discussion of what the likely core issue of their selected case might be and some help in refining and concretizing the case. For example, studying airline mergers in general is of limited relevance for a case study, but recommending *Lufthansa* to acquire *TAP* makes for a concrete topic full of possibilities. One could also consider an IPO for *FC Bayern Munich* or the introduction of virtual reality glasses for the *Deutsche Museum*.

Executives' feedback is crucial for self-selected and hypothetical cases since no one knows what will happen nor what the optimal solution will be. Thus it became obvious that only executives either close to the case or experts in dealing with the relevant issues are in a position to make judgments in respect of the logic and the solution to the case. Neither super smart university professors nor highly experienced consultants can offer this specific experience and judgment. Only closely involved executives or experts can achieve maximum relevance and credibility on the issues. They can state what the particular company is likely to examine or whether and how they would act on with regard to a specific topic. The closer the executive is to the issue at hand, the better, e.g. if the case is *Lufthansa* considering acquiring *TAP* the leader of *Lufthansa*'s M&A department would be the perfect discussion partner. He or she would bring truly exciting insights and relevant experience, which would make the feedback for the case team extremely pertinent as well as useful and exciting.

Executives' interaction with students is in any case exciting. We had both witnessed many interactions between executives and students on presentations or in seminars and knew of the positive impact it had. But here was potential for even more fruitful exchanges if executives engaged directly with those issues and questions students had worked on in their self-selected case. It would be as if the student team had developed their case on behalf of the executive involved; as if the case selection was also conducted not only with the executive but for him. Readers of these paragraphs can imagine how valuable such executive feedback is on working out unresolved questions. We concluded this could become the highlight of the seminar assuming appropriate executives or experts could be found and would be willing to come and discuss the self-selected cases with the student teams.

Attractive presentation was crucial, not only as a learning objective but when inviting executives for feedback. Preparing a case study presentation which approximates as closely as possible to a real-world situation with a real executive is very different from writing up a case study for reading. Presenting to executives requires tailored preparation. This goes well beyond clear charts and good presentation style. The team must compose the most effective setup for their argumentation and recommendations. It should be as realistic as possible—a simulacrum of the business world. Student teams might role play being company task forces or consultants or investment bankers and field questions accordingly. The audience could also be assigned certain roles, such as CEO or CFO if they feel that these stakeholder interests are relevant to the solution, and the owner representative of the company could even be addressed specifically.

Optimal preparation support for such an experience must be provided because the seminar should not only stimulate the students but also make a positive impression on the executives. They appreciate presentations being crisp, clear and to the point. They prefer the key facts and figures over lengthy elaborations. However, students may not have had the experience of having to give a presentation under such circumstances. Appropriate techniques and approaches need to be practiced during the working out of the case, as well as the formulation of a precise case question and clarity about the core analyses and scope of the topic. Students should be able to present an executive summary no longer than one page and a possible solution to the case with a convincing and logical supporting argument in an appealing and pithy presentation.

Producing an executive summary on one page is an art most managers must learn in their career—the earlier the better. Top managers do not want detailed facts and figures nor lengthy arguments of variable relevance. They do not decide strategic questions on the basis of SWOT analyses or Porter models. These are relevant for the student team in understanding the case and context but they should not appear in presentations to executives. Only in rare instances are Porter models appropriate, e.g. if an executive wants to enter a business segment he is not familiar with. Most often executives want top down logic, i.e. the recommended decision up front with expected impact qualitatively described and quantified, followed by the logic leading to the recommendation. This line of argumentation does not apply any particular business concept nor a method studied in business schools. The best presentation has a storyline tailor-made to the decision taker and building on the relevant context of the case. Take the following example: let's suppose we recommend an IPO to *FC Bayern Munich* in order that they can raise money to buy more expensive players. First we determine that buying expensive players is most important for future success. We then argue and demonstrate in numbers that now is a great time to make an IPO and that alternative financing efforts would not raise as much money. We also analyze why an IPO has not been made so far—e.g. due to unwanted influence of owners on sports decisions. For this specific issue there is a new solution with a precedent at other clubs that have IPOed successfully and established good governance, as in the case of several English soccer clubs. Such a line of argument would compose a top down storyline crisply and effectively underlining the recommendation. What students tend to do, on the other hand, is work out the pros and cons of IPOs compared to alternative financing methods, the options available to *FC Bayern Munich* to improve their existing resources, rounded off with and balancing lots of arguments based on the experience of other top clubs' IPOs, such as *Borussia Dortmund*. This may be followed by a chapter on governance of sports clubs by members and owners. One needs a lot of these analyses and arguments to come to a final recommendation. However, this is not going to make for an effective presentation of the case if communicated as such. We were thus convinced of the benefits of educating the student teams in these skills. Students should learn to present a one page as executives would expect them to in the real world. This would provide practical training in building the bridge from business management theory to real business life situations.

Executive feedback is crucial in arriving at the best case logic and solution. This objective is mandatory in particular for open cases and should result from an extensive Q&A session with the executive immediately after the presentation of the case. Student teams should answer questions from the executive with their backup calculations and detail their arguments on request. They also should receive feedback on missing arguments, more relevant insights and on plausible assumptions and check on the logic of their argumentation. With this feedback the case material and solution for the written case will be a lot closer to reality.

Writing up the case is another important part of learning through case studies. The techniques are well documented and there is a lot of good guidance easy to find in literature. The challenge would be to produce written cases that win case writing competitions from *EFMD*. EFMD is searching for exciting cases by case topics and seek a convincing logic and argumentation. We dreamt of winning such competitions and gaining international exposure. We had no clue whether and when that would happen, however the expectation was set from the very beginning.

The **time plan and procedure** for the advanced case study seminar was roughly set up; it was, however, obvious that these new approaches would need some field testing followed by fine-tuning. Thus written feedback from students after each seminar/each semester would be required and all participants in teaching would then synthesize the students' feedback and their own observations with a view to continuously improving each seminar.

2 Conclusion

The renewed advanced case study seminar had clear objectives: practice oriented and stimulating seminars for students, teaching staff motivated to support them intensively and committed to continuously improving the seminar, and last but not least, all visiting executives and experts should be positively impressed by the case study performance, the students' capabilities and thus the *TUM School of Management* approach. Every now and then there should be a winning team in international case writing competitions—and if the total format becomes as successful as desired, it might justify published documentation.

3 Solution

After 4 years and eight semesters, 80 student teams had experienced the case study seminar by mid-2017. The procedure and time plan for the seminar were well established as were the roles and contributions from the teachers and supporting tutors. Executives, although involved in very different cases, lauded the approach and several of them returned more than once. Feedback from the students has been extremely positive and two have recently received awards for case study writing. The specifics are detailed below.

The **time plan and procedures** of the advanced case seminar have been fine-tuned over the years and are now working well. Bachelor's and Master's students can enroll on the seminar—there are no prerequisites in terms of other courses. The students tend to apply early in their studies to secure a place in the oversubscribed seminar. After the selection of 30 students from a long list of those interested (typically two to three times oversubscribed), they meet in a kickoff session. Purpose and procedures as well as evaluation and timing/dates are imparted. Tutors and teachers introduce themselves and clarify their role and contributions in the seminar. The overview of major activities is shown in Fig. 1.

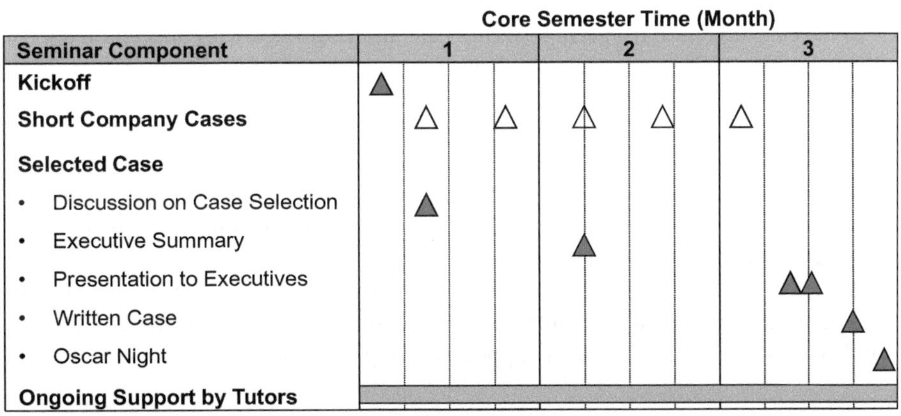

Fig. 1 Modern case study seminar—time plan

Kickoff content involves teaching students how to select and approach case studies. Typical learning material on formulating the core question, relevant issues and selected analyses as well as inductive logic are introduced—as in most case seminars (literature). Unique to this seminar is the case selection triggering. Students are encouraged to think of different case categories and in each of these case categories the key analyses used in practice are briefly mentioned. This is demonstrated with some examples.

IPOs is one category of cases. However, the seminar does not consider IPOs in hindsight but rather those that might come up in the future, such as an IPO for *FC Bayern Munich* or IPOs that are predicted in press articles like *snapchat* or *Zalando* (selected at the time before they IPOed). For IPOs it is crucial to have a convincing equity story and solid argumentation as to why the public market is the better owner of a company. Likewise, preparation and timing and a well thought out procedure for an IPO are requisite. As in the real world, the readiness, stability and the outlook of the company are important. A rough valuation of the offering has to be calculated and set in perspective against similar companies listed recently and compared to the market capital of peer competitors. Perspectives from all stakeholders are crucial and in several cases alternatives to an IPO may be added. A strategic sell off may be a better option if a strategic acquirer could generate more value than public ownership.

Another major category of cases is M&A. Obviously there must be a strategic expectation for a merger or any acquisition or sell off. This has to be verified with a deep understanding of the synergies expected. These are crucial for the outcome, the valuation and decision taking—underlining and quantifying the strategic argumentation. In complementary mergers, the additional sales expected should be detailed, and in consolidating mergers of similar companies the cost synergies and their capture is to be assessed well. Synergies and their realistic implementation also define the price offering that makes sense. In some open situations, one can also apply a reverse calculation, i.e. what synergies need to be achieved at bottom line in order to justify a realistic markup over market capital (for listed companies). Comparisons with similar recent mergers in the respective industry are useful in arriving at plausible assumptions about achievable synergies and for pricing evaluations.

In the case selection triggering, startups are also promoted with the central part of a business plan and the core players. Both are of huge importance to investors. They must be detailed and fit to realistic market and competitive assessments. Additionally, individuals' CVs and also financing plans as well as exit ideas are needed.

In mature industries, typical strategic questions are raised for companies focusing on their renewal and innovation efforts. As with all strategic questions they need a clear understanding of the economic benefits and quantitative impact. This is crucial for executives wrestling with strategic options.

At the end of the kickoff, students form ten teams of three each and start to exchange their views on their most exciting case ideas. They can discuss this for roughly two weeks until the next support meeting.

Discussion on case selection is done team by team in sessions with the student team, the assigned tutor who is a doctoral candidate at the department, and with Dr. Biagosch who brings his consultancy experience to the team. The student team may have already selected a preference or they come with two/three alternative case topics. While discussing and supporting the team in its selection a couple of important elements are focused on. Firstly, there must be true intellectual curiosity and excitement about the selected case. Secondly, it is preferred that the team has access to data and insights into the company concerned in the case. In particular, dealing with open cases for non-publishing companies it is helpful to have effective information sources. Some teams choose a company they had an internship at or were working at on a part time basis. Thirdly, the case formulation must involve critical issues and be solvable within a reasonable timeframe and workload.

What student teams finally select as cases is of particular interest—compare Fig. 2. The majority of cases are about corporate strategy although along various trajectories. The most popular category of cases, 19 of 80, dealt with technology-based expansions including those arising from internet or digitalization opportunities. Among these are several cases dealing with *BMW*'s *iSeries* and electric cars, and *Tesla*'s infrastructure building, as well as companies like *Aldi*, *Lidl* or *Fielmann* looking to establish online businesses. These selections are to be expected at *TUM* since many students have a background in natural sciences or engineering or IT. The second most selected case category is expansion strategies into new business segments—e.g. airlines entering low-cost long range flights, or companies planning regional expansions and entry into other business segments. Other corporate strategy topics involve defensive strategies against competition,

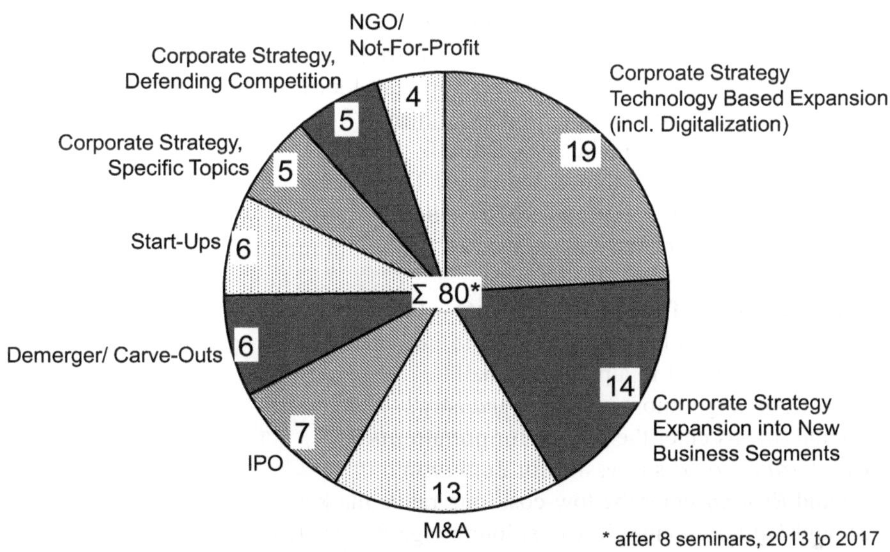

Fig. 2 Case selection by student teams—number of cases 2013–2017

very specific company topics such as *Unicredit's* outsourcing of finance processing, or the *BMW-Apple* collaboration on automobiles. Thirteen cases had to do with M&As such as *Lufthansa* acquiring other airlines (or not) and *Siemens* buying *Gamesa* (selected before it actually happened). There were also six demergers or carve-outs, such as the splitting up of *eon* and options for *BMW* to carve out its electric vehicles or *BMW iServices*. Seven case teams worked on IPOs–*FC Bayern Munich*, *snapchat* and *Zalando*, each before the actual IPO happened. Six teams selected startup companies either in the very early stages before funding (*Co-Living* as a premium flat-sharing community) or they selected growth strategies for advancing businesses like *mymuesli* and *freeletics*. Only four cases were picked concerning NGOs/Not-for-Profit Organizations such as the *Deutsche Museum*, *TUM* or *State Opera of Bavaria*.

Students' Case Selection
***Corporate Strategy* . . .**

. . .with expansion based on technology (incl. digitalization)—19 cases
- Is *BMW* better off with lithium-ion batteries or fuel cells?
- *BMW iSeries*—can additional services enhance profitability of the EV segment?
- Should *BMW* cooperate with *Tesla* in electric loading infrastructure?
- How should *Tesla* build-up infrastructure in Europe?
- Should *Tesla* build up infrastructure captive or in cooperation?
- Should *Siemens* invest in Hyperloop?
- First pilot of Hyperloop in Germany (*Siemens*)
- *eon* business model for storage systems with private households
- Should *eon* invest in electrical loading infrastructure?
- Should *Drive Now* switch its fleet into electrical?
- Should *Retech* enter market for surgical instrument disinfection systems?
- Should *Lidl* introduce online services for fresh food?
- Should *Aldi-Süd* enter online food retail market?
- *Fielmann* to enter online business like *Mr. Spex*? (**2**)
- E-ticketing for *MVV* (Munich Municipal Transportation)
- *Kuka's* chance in the 4th industrial revolution
- Fintechs—should banks engage in? (**2**)

. . .with expansion of business segments—14 cases
- Volkswagen—market entry into China low-cost? (**2**)
- Should *Audi* invest in a plant in Brazil?
- Should *Apple* go into automotive industry?
- Should *Airbus* enter the market for private jets?
- Can *Eurowings* be successful for *Lufthansa*?
- Should *Ryanair* enter the low-cost long range market?
- Should *Lufthansa* enter low-cost long range flights? (**2**)
- Potential for a softdrink to *Adidas*
- Should *FC Bayern Munich* go international?

- Should *Hermes* enter the letter business?
- Should *eon* expand into regional networks?
- *Flixbus*—expansion into US market?

. . .**M&A—13 cases**
- *Lufthansa* acquiring government owned *TAP*
- Should *Lufthansa* acquire *SAS*?
- Should *Lufthansa* acquire *Turkish Airlines*?
- *AirBerlin*—target for *Lufthansa*?
- Should *Daimler* buy *Tesla*?
- Should *Vokswagen* buy *Ashok Leyland*?
- Should *Siemens* buy *Nordex*?
- Should *ZF* acquire *TRW*?
- Is *Linde*'s acquisition of *Lincare* a masterpiece or fruitless expansion?
- Is *Facebook* best owner for *WhatsApp* or *Google*?
- *UBS* acquisition of *Commerzbank*?
- How should *Meditrade* improve its recent acquisition (PMM)?
- *Siemens* merger with *Gamesa*

. . .**IPO—7 cases**
- IPO of *FC Bayern Munich* (**2**)
- Should *Zalando* go public?
- *Bubble.com*—IPO or cooperation with publishing house?
- Should *snapchat* IPO?
- *Flixbus*—exit strategies for *General Atlantic*?
- IPO or not—how should *Caribou Biosciences* finance its growth?

. . .**Demerger/Carve-outs—6 cases**
- Evaluate *eon*'s splitting in two companies (**2**)
- Should *Airbus* sell its defense business?
- Should *BMW* carve-out its *iServices*?
- Should *BMW* carve-out its electric vehicle division?
- Should *Siemens* divest *Healthineers*?

. . .**Start-ups—6 cases**
- *Unu* e-scooter sharing for conquering European markets
- *Wearables*—an upcoming opportunity for health insurers?
- Growth strategy for *mymuesli*
- *Freeletics*—disrupting the fitness industry
- Develop a growth strategy for *miBaby*
- *Co-Living* extending business in Munich

. . .**Corporate strategy, specific topics—5 cases**
- Can *Volkswagen* beat *Toyota* without further M&A?
- The future of *eon*'s Irsching power plant

- Cooperation from *BMW* and *Apple* in automobiles
- Should *German Government* abolish fixed prices for drugs?
- *Unicredit*—outsourcing of finance processing
- *Deutsche Post* with *Streetscooter*—future commercialization strategy

... **defending competition—5 cases**
- How can *Adidas* defend *Under Armors* entering in the European market?
- *Siemens* mobility divisions success against Chinese competition
- How can *Intel* defend its new strategy?
- New perspective for *Siemens* energy business
- How can a small Bavarian brewery survive in the German beer market?

... **NGO/Not-for-profit—4 cases**
- Financial improvement of the *Bavarian State Opera*
- Financing perspectives of *TUM*
- Should *Deutsches Museum* invest into virtual reality?
- *Deutsches Museum*—how to create new space and how to finance it?

Almost all cases had future business opportunities in mind and most were strategic in nature. Very few cases had restructuring or operations efforts as a topic and organisational effectiveness was rarely selected. This all indicates that the active creation of business opportunities is by far the most attractive topic. Also attractive are famous companies like *Siemens*, *BMW*, *Lufthansa*, *VW-Group* and *eon* plus *FC Bayern Munich*. *TUM* students seem more interested in these than in financial institutions or healthcare companies—compare Fig. 3.

The **executive summary discussion** is a core element of learning for the student teams. Each team has to prepare a one pager with a synthesis of their planned executive presentation and discuss this with Dr. Biagosch, who is very familiar

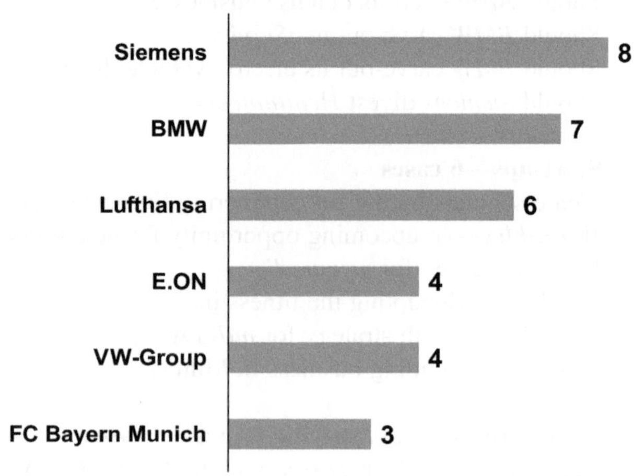

Fig. 3 Case selection by student teams—most involved companies

with one pagers, which are a standard basis for executive discussions at board level where time is limited. Consultants typically call this "the elevator story" when you meet the CEO in an elevator by chance and you only have a couple of floors to tell him the status and likely outcome of your work. One needs to avoid going into too much detail, even if this is presented in a structured format. Likely outcomes—maybe formulated as a hypothesis and a top down argumentation—need to be presented with the key underlining facts. Here is a very short example:

> *Volkswagen* should buy *Alfa Romeo* if it is sold by *FCA* for a reasonable price. The key reason is that *Volkswagen Group* has the platforms and technologies in *Porsche* and *Audi* ready for *Alfa's* use and thus can revitalize the *Alfa* brand faster than *FCA*. *Alfa* employees have already reacted positively to the possibility of belonging to *Volkswagen Group* rather than to *FCA*. If *FCA* wants to focus on its target volume, *Alfa* could be sold and "paid for" with *SEAT*, which has five times the *Alfa* volume today and fits better to *FCA* (*SEAT's* origin was *FIAT*). This would allow *FCA* to reach their volume and financial targets a lot faster and cheaper. Due diligence of both companies under each other's proposed ownership would be advisable as the next step.

Student teams have some difficulty synthesizing and coming up with short and effective messages. They tend to deliver what they have examined and they structure it in a procedural or topical way rather than using top down messaging. The preparation of executive summaries using top down logic is crucial for a good presentation and one of the most important aspects of training.

The four **short company case studies** also concentrate on this training when student teams have to present their recommendation after a very short information input and reflection time. The more crisply they can deliver the message and the fewer but relevant facts one delivers, the better. As preparation for management discussions the selection and sequencing of facts and data is decisive. There is a common saying that it requires maximum talent and logic to be short and to the point as opposed to long-winded and thorough.

The **presentations to executives** are the highlight of the case study seminar. To find and convince the appropriate person on the specific case is difficult but worth the effort. E.g. for the *Lufthansa* acquisitions, the head of M&A, Mr. Nettesheim, came to discuss the cases a couple of times. Likewise *BMW*'s executive from their strategic department, Mr. Muster, often supported students on *BMW* cases. Several *Siemens* strategists from different divisions participated, and from *E.ON*, Mr. Bohrer, the head of sales coordination came several times. In startup cases the founders of the company came and in critical strategic discussions involved *McKinsey & Company* experts helped—in particular when company representatives were not allowed to argue open cases publicly. This also happened in IPO cases when involved executives were legally not allowed to come and speak. However, closely linked experts could. In one case we were not even allowed to publish the team's findings because they could potentially harm an important planned action. The unplanned and more value creating solution was not appreciated by a major owner. Such issues are expected in open and future cases with their potential public interest and the faculty will deal with this appropriately.

The presentations typically take 30 min and the Q and A and feedback takes another 30 min. We have each one of the student teams of three present one part, and we have our executive or expert and four other teams plus all tutors in the room when this happens. This enables other students to learn from their colleagues' experiences. This format is also effective when two teams have selected the same or similar topics, e.g. two *Hyperloop* cases. Two approaches to the same topic is also interesting and useful for our executive guests—in particular when they travel to Munich. Presenting to executives is the best motivator for the student teams to come with well thought through presentations and they typically deliver with great passion. They receive specific feedback and bespoke answers to their questions. Many teams use role plays, e.g. setting the presentation with intros like "the board asked us to examine..." or "we as investment bankers recommend the shareholders IPO..." Some also bring product examples or embed videos in their presentation. Together with the case selection and the case logic, the presentation in itself is the third evaluation criterion.

Oscar Night is what we call the meeting where we convene over a beer and review the cases and their presentations jointly with the whole faculty and all the students. We nominate the best cases in three categories: Case selection, case logic and case presentation. Often we have three case teams nominated in each category. It is important to argue specifically for why a team should be nominated. In case selection, one could be nominated for innovativeness such as a pitch for a startup, or for complexity and difficulty as with the new *Intel* strategy, or for novelty in the seminar as with the *Fintech* case. Case logic is nominated for effectiveness and completeness of argumentation that also impresses the visiting executive "like *UBS* acquires *Commerzbank*"—a *UBS* strategist and other bankers were involved in appraising the thoughts of the team. Presentations can be most effective when creative approaches are applied. For example, in a beer brewery survival case study, the team created newly designed bottles and beer for the presentation. The marketing effect was very realistic although content wise the case solution did not convince the senior executive. He was a former CEO of several brewery companies who had been behind a number of restructurings and mergers. He liked the teams' appearance but based on his experience did not agree that the proposed solution would work.

The whole faculty votes to find the winner from the nominated teams and the prizes are recognition, good grades and bottles of wine. Oscar Night is intended to help all teams reflect on and learn from their experiences.

The **written case study** embeds the executives' feedback. In all 80 cases so far, the feedback has improved the case study significantly and sometimes it has even led to a reversal of the recommendation. This is understandable because student teams obviously do not have executive level judgment and experience. In particular, for open/future cases, facts and figures must be guessed and could be wrong, or the requisite business experience is simply missing. Examples are bottom up calculations e.g. for internet deliveries from *Lidl*; we learned that storage, item picking, rejection rates and deliveries are altogether too costly, and in relation to these the average purchase volumes are too small to generate profits. This meant that the recommendation was negative and the expansion into the internet is currently not even worth piloting. Future cost reductions and/or productivity gains may change that recommendation. Likewise the margins of *Fielmann* glasses from their shops are so high that an online business for *Fielmann* similar to that of *Mister Spex* would diminish the average margin—thus a *Fielmann* online business should certainly not happen under the *Fielmann* brand. Different judgments can come with different risk assessment like the *UBS* being afraid of asset risks within *Commerzbank* and values this impact higher than the student team did anticipate. Organizational experience and judgment was also against a carve-out of *BMW iSeries* because a carve-out format would be less effective, less fast and less courageous than doing it within the established *BMW* organization and with support from the executive board. Again an experience, only involved executives can judge on. This is most exciting for the students to learn from the practical world.

Student feedback from the seminars has improved over the sessions held in recent years. It was always highly rated and has subsequently become one of the top performing courses at *TUM School of Management*. Figure 4 shows a recent evaluation and indicates quantitatively and qualitatively very high levels of satisfaction. On a scale of 1–5 (1 being best), the overall score for the seminar including the students' perceived benefit and the quality of the teacher is between 1.2 and 1.4. Among more specific valuations, top ratings were achieved on the concept, structure, execution and teachers' qualifications. Also top ratings were given for the students' learning in terms of competence and for their leadership experience in practical business life. The ratings for the overall difficulty (2.8), and the contribution to scientific work and credits given (both 2.2) are good. Although the workload is high, students appreciate the self-selection of the case, the ongoing concrete support and

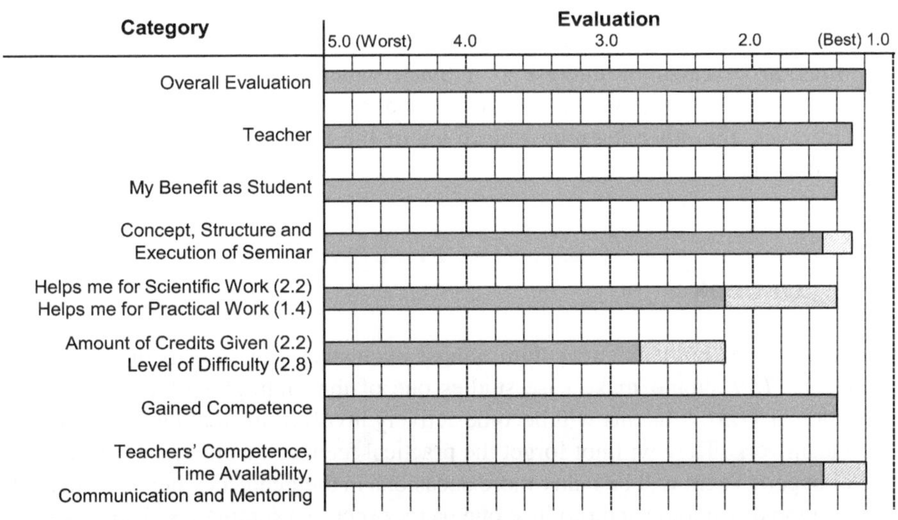

Fig. 4 Student feedback on the case seminar—synthesis (Winter Semester 2016/2017)

For almost thirty years, *EFMD* has been organizing this case writing competition by the **Case Center**. Through the competition *EFMD* encourages and supports the writing and creation of new and innovative case material. The cases deal with topics generally under-represented among the available sources.

2016 edition winners include:

1) Finance and Banking, sponsored by *Toulouse Business School*

"UBS: Acquisition of Commerzbank AG as a possible growth strategy" written by:

- Philipp Deisler, Technical University of Munich, DE
- Michael Eisenlauer, Technical University of Munich, DE
- Fahrudin Abazi; Technical University of Munich, DE

2) Urban Transition Challenges, sponsored by *Climate Kic*

"unu GmbH: Sharing is caring – a suitable business model for e-scooters in Germany?" written by:

- Frieder Johann Weidenbach, Technical University of Munich, DE
- Franziska Beck, Technical University of Munich, DE
- Michael Krauss; Technical University of Munich, DE

We would like to warmly congratulate all of the winners and once again thank all of our sponsors for their continued support of the *EFMD* Case Writing Competition.

Fig. 5 EFMD case writing competition (Source: www.efmd.org)

the executives' feedback being truly specific to their case. It can be assumed that this case study seminar remains one of the best experiences in students' education. Typical quotes are "best course of my studies so far" or "feels very close to reality and is exciting". Even cases where the original recommendation was rejected by the executive or expert are likely to be remembered positively—maybe even exceptionally well.

Winning case writing competitions is relatively recent but provides inspiration for further successes. Two cases took first place at *EFMD* rankings—see Fig. 5. The award for the students and the reputation boost for the *TUM School of Management* are encouraging. Although winning is not so important that case selection would be influenced and tailored to the competition demands, it nevertheless serves as a nice confirmation of cases of interest to a much wider group of professionals and universities and is a testament to very good case logic and convincing write up. However, the other learning objectives of the case study seminar remain of higher importance.

4 Outlook

As *Harvard* has built its curriculum almost exclusively on case method teaching seminars, *TUM* should make case studies one of the highlights of their students' education at *TUM*. Students will become actively involved in creating their case and learn teamwork. They will not forget the practical feedback from the chosen executive or expert. There will be many more occasions in their careers when students will draw on top down logic and produce one pager executive summaries. They also feel the benefit of dry runs before presentations and they will again seek insights from experts before recommending their own solutions because they see that the case can be better argued in content and logic and in key assumptions.

The *TUM* and the School of Management faculty will continue improving the seminar further, e.g. add a special kickoff for writing the case or adjust the amount of work from students and offer more credits.

Other departments at other universities may adopt some of the good practices pioneered here and establish their own case study seminars along the same lines. This is certain to be appreciated because modern case seminars are an important and effective bridge between theoretical learning and real world business practice. So far the format is unique to the *TUM*, but we are sure that faculties and students everywhere would appreciate a broader rollout.

Supporting Companies and Participating Managers in Case Study Presentations

Andreas Biagosch

In the following, those companies and individuals are listed that supported students with self-selected case studies. More often than not, they are from the case study company or at least involved in the case defined. The individuals typically represent functions and leadership positions closest to the case topics.

All participating managers attended the presentations and gave specific feedback—a few participated via video conference. Their comments reflected the actual thinking of the company, its division, or special function with respect to the case. Obviously, guests could and would not disclose company secrets, where cases are real and discussions ongoing. In all discussions the feedback significantly improved the case logic and its argumentation—sometimes even causing the recommendation to be reversed. Thus it is of huge value for student teams to share their presentation and enter into a dialogue with executives and experts. The teams regularly received specific insights and judgements from the real world, e.g. founders of startups with their likes and dislikes, large company perspectives based on their owners' experiences (e.g. with respect to mergers), or comments leading to even better options than the case recommendation in respect of future investments. While all contributions are extremely welcome, they could not all be listed here, and so we include a very short selection of exemplary inputs. These should give the reader an idea of the discussion in certain cases.

In the name of the participating students, student teams with their cases, and the faculty staff we would like to thank the following participants for their most valuable contributions.

Adidas—Dino Dario Monopoli from New Product Development appreciated the soft drink "sportdrink" idea for *Adidas* and he greatly improved the students'

A. Biagosch (✉)
Technical University of Munich, Munich, Germany
e-mail: biagosch@impacting1.com

G. Friedl, A. Biagosch (eds.), *Case Studies in Strategic Management*,
Management for Professionals, https://doi.org/10.1007/978-3-319-95555-1_2

thinking in the case of "how *Adidas* should defend *Under Armour*". We learned how deeply one needs to understand a company's marketing strength and focus.

Allianz—Jan Wiedemann contributed a realistic perspective on the extent to which wearable tracking devices can affect health insurance policies. Adapting insurance policies to data from wearables actually turned out to be a lot more difficult than originally thought. However, wearables are useful in gathering health information and warnings as fast as possible.

Bavarian Opera—Dr. Roland Schwab as leading director of the opera house shared the team's ideas on improving its economic situation to become as successful as the *Metropolitan Opera* in New York—except agreeing to a ball like the famous Vienna Opera Ball.

BMW—Bernd Muster, Lorenz Rein and Markus Bartenschlager from *BMW Strategy*, head of Product Marketing Car Sharing and project leader for Charge Now, contributed several times on *BMW*'s priorities with respect to brand strengthening vs. activities any OEM could provide. They also clarified to what extent *BMW* can benefit from *Apple*'s strengths and reviewed carve-out options for new *iBMW* services critically. They also discussed whether *DriveNow* should switch to electric vehicles given its challenging economics.

Co-Living—Ferdinand von Fumetti (*Co-Living*) and Robert Gallenberger from *b-to-v* (Venture Capital) helped evaluate the expansion of an apartment sharing service for young people with high incomes. What works in Berlin could work even better in Munich due to its very high rents.

Daimler AG—Matthias Grun clarified the *Daimler-Tesla* involvements and interactions, as well as their disengagement. He also supported a team working on mobility services with respect to organic growth and acquisitions.

Deutsches Museum—Prof. Dr. Wolfgang Heckl and Sabine Schulz-Hammerl welcomed the students' ideas on applying VR in the museum and on new financing ideas for the so-called "forum"—a center focusing on the latest technological innovations. It turned out that there are more great ideas than there is financing.

Deutsche Post—Armin Haas helped in calculating logistical costs effectively and judging a possible entry of *Hermes* into private post business. The solution, apparently, is not (yet) a good one.

DHL—Uwe Horn supported the general idea of delivery services even for discounters. These are slowly growing with decreasing costs of dispatch and delivery.

Earlybird—Dr. Hendrik Brandis as an expert in venture capital and internet businesses highlighted the important cash needs behind *Zalando*'s IPO and commented on best owners for *WhatsApp* (before it was sold) as well as on the *snapchat* IPO and its valuation. The evaluation of loss making internet companies is a very special topic.

E.ON—Rainer Bohrer supported teams three times on *eon*'s split up effects, the continuation of the world's most efficient power plant in Irsching, despite a closure plan, and the development of an electric storage system for households.

E.ON—Christoph Somborn commented on *eon*'s entry into e-car charging infrastructure in Germany and its special economics.

FC Bayern—Prof. Dr. Herbert Henzler as longtime member of the board was able to comment specifically on two IPO cases from the *FC Bayern* owners' and club members' view. It became clear why it has not happened yet despite originally being recommended by both teams.

Fielmann-online—Oliver Bücken not a *Fielmann* representative, but investor and Business Angel with experience in the industry reminded the team of the enormous brand value of *Fielmann* and the danger of losing this partly in (pure) online business.

Fintech and online startups—Dr. Marc-Henning Diekmann and Dr. Arnold Bahlmann lent their support in assessing a *Buddybank* startup idea and growth financing for *Babbel* as language learning App. As with all startup pitches the questions end in an honest answer whether one would invest money in it.

Flixbus—André Schwämmlein as one of the founders shared his view about *Flixbus* IPO and alternative strategic options/strategic partnerships. The learning was that rational arguments may not be compatible with emotive aspects and perspectives of founders.

Freeletics—Daniel Sobhani and Stephan Hauner as owners appreciated the growth ideas for their successful sports app on fitness improvement, but reminded the team of the need for careful selection and priorization of opportunities on which young companies need to focus.

Infineon—Dr. Andreas Schumacher as leading strategist of the successful semi-conductor company helped evaluate the new *Intel* strategy, which is somewhat at odds with typical disintegration trends in the semiconductor industry.

KUKA—Thomas Delaforge contributed to a strategic perspective on *KUKA*'s future regarding new products and services, in particular concerning the "fourth industrial revolution". A good quantification of digitalization effects is difficult to do—in particular from outside in.

Lufthansa—Marc-Dominic Nettesheim has now visited the faculty five times. He specified and tailored the low cost carrier ideas from *Eurowings* and long distance carriers, and argued specifically on potential mergers of *LH* with *SAS*, *TAP* and *Turkish Airlines*. None of the mergers proposed have happened—so far. Airline business with sold seat passenger revenue vs. cost rules continues to attract student teams.

McKinsey—Georg Bundy helped evaluate an *Apple* car as connected car. At this point in time, everybody expected an *Apple* Car to have been launched.

McKinsey—Volker Grüntges has visited the faculty four times. As an automotive expert he commented on the likely prospects for *Volkswagen*'s low cost segment—maybe with an acquisition in China. He supported the idea for *Volkswagen's* acquisition of *Alfa Romeo*. Two other cases were the likely strategy with respect to electrification and battery sourcing, and the option of an *Audi* plant in South America.

McKinsey—Dr. Arnt-Philipp Hein contributed on the competitiveness in rail systems, in particular *Siemens* versus Chinese competitors. With local specifications and innovations the cost gap may be reduced if not closed completely.

McKinsey—Dr. Detlef Kayser commented on perspectives in the wind energy sector, e.g. *Siemens* acquisition of *Nordex*—not recommended. This happened before the *Gamesa* case came up—in the seminar and in reality.

McKinsey—Dr. Philipp Radtke contributed on the possibility of *Volkswagen* truck division acquiring *Ashok Leyland* from India as low cost player. It may be a good idea for *Volkswagen* but not (yet) for the owners of *Ashok Leyland*.

McKinsey—Dr. Markus Schmid as consumer expert clarified risks and prospects in the fresh food delivery services and delivery services for discounters—growing slowly due to high costs.

McKinsey—Wolff van Sintern helped in several cases, e.g. *Airbus* spin-off of its defense business, *Siemens-Gamesa* merger, and whether *Airbus* should enter private business jets. The aerospace and defense industry has its own rules.

Meditrade—Martin Unterberg of *Meditrade* appreciated the team's integration plan for a newly acquired business in medtech products. The team worked as a consultant to *Meditrade*, who disclosed the situation openly to them.

miBaby—Dr. Björn Anton and Dr. Tim Kettenring as founders of the startup for young mothers commented on the team's growth and expansion ideas and focused on priorities versus trying everything with their small team.

mymuesli—Patrick Huber from *mymuesli* not only tailored the team's ideas on the growth of the individual muesli businesses, he also invited the seminar participants to visit their plant in Passau.

Siemens Healthcare—Dr. Christoph Windpassinger gave feedback on the IPO of *Siemens Healthcare Division* long before it appeared in the press.

Siemens Mobility—Bernhard Kuderer and Armin Haupt discussed the *Hyperloop* ideas and first business introductions with a view to *Siemens* participating—so far unlikely to be realized despite the successful prototype from a *TUM* team.

Siemens P&C—Sören Buttkereit clarified many specifications and assumptions in the acquisition of *Dresser Rand*. The synergies play a critical role but cannot overcompensate external market effects currently not playing well for this acquisition.

Siemens Rail—Karin Knör from its strategy department could specifically evaluate all ideas of *Siemens Rail* to compete successfully against the very strong Chinese competition. Several ideas for future tenders were exchanged.

Special Beer Brewery—Dr. Jobst Kayser-Eichberg being truly experienced in the development of small and specialized breweries brought a realistic perspective to the team's ideas and underlined the continuing consolidation trend in the industry. Specialties can help, but not fully change the consolidation towards huge entities.

StreetScooter—Prof. Achim Kampker evaluated the future exit ideas for the successful electric commercial vehicle from the *RWTH Aachen*. Its origination at the University and now *Deutsche Post* ownership does not necessarily imply that it will continue successfully without a strong partner.

SWM, MVG—Andreas Mattivi and Lars Küttner leading Munich's Infrastructure and Passenger Transportation System were able to argue the difficulties in modernizing electronic ticketing and payment systems taking all users' (in)capabilities into account. E-ticketing is a costly add-on option and cannot immediately substitute existing systems adequately.

Tesla—Christian Zeh from *Tesla* helped with realistic assumptions while building up a fast charging infrastructure in Europe for long distance travel with full electric vehicles.

TUM—Albert Berger, Chancellor of *TUM* contributed on innovative ideas concerning financing of special services of a modern university. We learned a lot about models—some of them already applied at *TUM*.

UBS—Sebastian Görres and Markus Hermainski as strategist and director from the bank appreciated the thoughts of the team but did not rate the chance and risk balance in favor of the acquisition and reversed the original recommendation of the team. For more information, please read the case study in this book.

UniCredit—Dirk Hoppmann gave insights into the difficult topic of IT outsourcing and IT offshoring of an established bank. A challenging aspect for a bank that cannot be compared with greenfield solutions.

UnternehmerTUM—Andreas Unseld and Dr. Ingo Potthof commented on startups and venture financing including exit options for *Caribou Biosciencs* with their CRISPR-CAS 9 development, and on pharmacies pricing against internet pharmacies. Mr. Potthof argued on *Flixbus* exit options from an investor's point of view.

unu—Pascal Blum as founder appreciated the thorough and deep-going analyses of the team on the *unu* scooters with respect to brand differentiating and sharing economy trends. For more information please read the case study in this book.

ZF—Dr. Holger Klein as leader of the integration team was able to illuminate the *TRW* acquisition and strategic perspective for *ZF* as well as the PMM (Post Merger Management).

The reader may have realized that there were some strategic cases or IPOs where experts participated rather than the executives from the case company. The reason is obvious: for confidentiality reasons executives cannot comment on a planned or upcoming IPO nor on a new strategy or merger that has not yet been disclosed to the public and to all shareholders. In these cases, experts close to the case help and can give feedback which is congruent with insiders' views.

Once again, a huge thank you to all participants. Their contributions were hugely appreciated by the student teams. Executives' engagement in students' education is always highly valued and most effective, if they contribute very specifically to students' case work.

Case: unu GmbH: Sharing Is Caring—A Suitable Business Model for E-Scooter in Germany

Franziska Beck, Michael Krauß, and Frieder Weidenbach

Abbreviations

app	Application
B2B	Business-to-Business
B2C	Business-to-Consumer
CEO	Chief Executive Officer
ct.	cent
CO_2	Carbon dioxide
CXO	Chief Officer
€	Euro
e-scooter	Electric scooter
h	hour
JV	Joint venture
1 k	One thousand
km	Kilometers
1 m	One million
min	minute
unu	unu GmbH
$	US Dollar
V	Volt

Submitted by: Franziska Beck, Michael Krauß, Frieder Weidenbach
Reviewer: Prof. Dr. Gunther Friedl, Verena Limbrunner.

F. Beck (✉) · M. Krauß · F. Weidenbach
Technical University of Munich, Munich, Germany
e-mail: franziska.beck@tum.de

G. Friedl, A. Biagosch (eds.), *Case Studies in Strategic Management*,
Management for Professionals, https://doi.org/10.1007/978-3-319-95555-1_3

1 Introduction

On 15th September 2015 Pascal Blum (CEO) and Elias Atahi (CXO), founder of unu GmbH (unu), drove home from Munich to their new office in Berlin. Coming from an exhausting but fruitful strategy workshop, where possible growth opportunities for the young startup had been discussed, Pascal and Elias were very happy and confident in their young team and their productive suggestions. In particular, the idea of electric scooter (e-scooter) sharing as a second branch sounded very exciting to them as it would complement unu's core business. Both shared the opinion that this idea should be followed in the near future. So they assigned further analysis of a potential business plan to their business development team.

1.1 unu GmbH

Maybe the location of Munich, where everything began, had a positive influence on the team. Here two graduates of the Technical University of Munich founded unu in 2013 with the support of Silicon Valley investor Michael Baum as well as the business angels Michael Hoeck and Maximilian Thyssen, who have expertise in the automotive and e-commerce business.[1] Both are very grateful, because without the help they would not be where they are now.

unu is a producer of environmental-friendly scooters, which are designed to address the needs and concerns of young customers. The batteries which use the newest Lithium-Ion technology are special because of their easy portability. Changing the battery of the scooter is uncomplicated and quick. The battery has a carrying handle, which allows the user to take it home, where they can charge it on a normal 230 V electric socket. This takes about 5–6 h. The scooter also has space for a second battery. A scooter with one battery has a reach of 50 km and a scooter with two batteries can last up to 100 km.[2]

The unu business model (Fig. 1) is simple and provides carefree mobility to its customers. The customer can configure and order their individual e-scooter easily online with a few mouse clicks. In the next step the individualized scooter will be produced and then delivered directly to the customer's home. The customer can decide on an insurance package and a license plate, which comes with additional costs but enables the customer to use their scooter immediately after delivery. Following this business model there is no need to store the scooters and it provides a direct customer relationship for unu by excluding retailers.[3] unu operates as a platform and does not own many fixed assets. This allows unu to be very flexible and adapt to new challenges as they arise.[4] While they were driving on the highway Pascal and Elias shared their thoughts and both agreed that they were immensely

[1]See unu GmbH (2015a).

[2]See unu GmbH (2015b).

[3]See unu GmbH (2015c).

[4]See Blum (2015).

proud of their team and their faith in unu's values (Fig. 2). All of them live the culture of the startup, which is in their eyes the reason for their success and potential for growth: The support of barrier-free creativity and realization of upcoming ideas. In their opinion, there is always room for improvement, so they are always interested in finding simple solutions.[5]

1.2 Trends

The unu team challenges the status quo and is not afraid to tackle the big problems of the world, so they consider themselves as a David who can outperform Goliath.[6] That is why it is important for Pascal and Elias to be aware of current mega trends and find mobility solutions which address them (Fig. 3).

One mega trend is urbanization, whose consequence is the movement of people towards the cities. Within these urban areas, the volume of traffic is increasing drastically, resulting in a huge demand for dedicated parking space. Other mega trends such as individual mobility and environmental awareness should be mentioned, to which competitors in the automobile industry have reacted with a new trend towards e-mobility. People like to be flexible, but are also conscious about the environment. These trends are addressed in their innovative and environmentally friendly e-scooter.

The unu team has also identified the sharing economy as a very young but rapidly increasing trend. Within the last couple of years alone, more and more people in bigger cities have been using at least one of the car or bike sharing services. Therefore, the idea of e-scooter sharing would fit perfectly with this trend. From the beginning, Elias was passionate about the combination of their unu scooters and e-scooter sharing. All their values seemed to fit perfectly with the new concept.

1.3 Customer Needs

Trends are not the only important thing to consider. New ideas for business models also have to address potential customers. The unu team loves the city and wants to be connected to its people and places.[7] Following this principle, the analysis of unu's customer needs and potential new customers was not only important but essential (Fig. 4). Based on their survey results, Elias and Pascal knew that existing unu scooters customers were very satisfied with their purchase. They were aware of their support of an environmental-friendly mobility solution with cutting-edge e-scooter technology. Another enormous benefit for customers was that they no longer needed to search for any parking space. Elias was of the opinion that new customers could be found if they pursued the new sharing economy trend. People who live in a city favor

[5]See unu GmbH (2015a).

[6]See unu GmbH (2015a).

[7]See unu GmbH (2015a).

more flexibility and time and desire more affordable and less troublesome mobility solutions.

2 Business Model for E-Scooter Sharing

2.1 Business Model of E-Scooter Sharing for unu

Both Elias and Pascal liked the idea of providing a fully serviced, affordable and carefree mobility solution for their customers. They agreed that the business development team should follow this idea of e-scooter sharing (Fig. 5).

The fleet would have to have an adequate number of e-scooters to establish a foothold in the market. unu's aim was to enable the customer to reach a shared scooter in less than 10 min walk. Furthermore, the concept of free floating units was decided on, which allows non-station based usage of scooters. The scooters would be distributed and could be booked and parked everywhere in the operation area of the particular city. Of course, existing road traffic regulations apply. unu's scooters should be freely available 24 h a day, 7 days a week and from March to October.[8] During the winter months, unu would store the scooters in a rented storage depot, where the necessary maintenance, repair and overhaul for the next season of operation could be carried out. All equipment needed for use with a scooter would be available on board, including two helmets (size M and L) and single-use hygiene caps.

The registration and booking process was designed in the following way: The customer, who should already be in possession of a regular car or scooter driving license, has to register with unu first. This can be done online or personally at one of the registration offices. After registration, the user can book a scooter whenever wanted with unu's smartphone application (app). This booking process (Fig. 6) is based on already existing sharing apps and therefore should feel very intuitive for the customer. The customer can locate the nearest scooter with their smartphone and unlock it by entering the four-digit code displayed on the app. The helmet box can also be opened and the user can choose a helmet size of their choice and use a hygiene cap. The engine can be started without using a key. To finish the ride, the user only has to click on the button "finish the ride" on his smartphone app and enter the displayed code to lock the scooter again. Optionally, the customer can simply park the scooter and push the "parking" button on the app. The customer pays a fee to unu for each usage. The pricing model was kept simple so that the customer could quickly understand and select the tariffs. A complex pricing model would just deter new customers.

unu would take care of all other activities related to a fully covered service package. This would include charging, maintenance and insurance of the scooter fleet. unu would have employees who change empty batteries and charge them. Pascal thought of additional side benefits for unu. The sharing model was in his view

[8]The climate diagram of Berlin as an example for all German cities (Fig. 7) was taken into account.

also an optimal marketing tool for the core business, because unu scooters would be seen all around city, so potential buyers become aware of the product and could test drive it immediately.

2.2 Benchmarking

In order to derive a pricing model and to gain a better understanding of the market, Elias asked the task force to conduct a benchmarking analysis. To achieve broad overview, established car and bike sharing services as well as established international scooter sharing services were considered.

2.2.1 Car Sharing

There are many car sharing services operating in Germany but two very distinct players seemed useful for further evaluation: DriveNow, a 50/50 joint venture (JV) between BMW Group and Sixt SE[9] as well as Car2Go, a 75/25 JV between Daimler Group and Europcar Group.[10] Both service providers use a free floating system which is deemed to have the biggest potential in the future.[11] This means customers are not forced to pick up or return their car at or to a specific service point.[12] Car sharing in Germany has experienced a steep growth during the last few years, doubling the number of users and cars between 2012 and 2015 to over 15,000 cars and over 900,000 customers.[13] (Fig. 8)

DriveNow, founded in 2011, offers a relatively wide product range varying in car brand, size and engine type while applying per-minute and hourly price packages for its customers (Fig. 9). German cities, where the service is operated, include Munich (520 cars), Berlin (1080 cars), Düsseldorf (250 cars), Cologne (300 cars) and Hamburg (560 cars). The origin of operation was Berlin with 250 cars and was able to attract 30,000 customers within its first 15 months. In 2015, DriveNow had more than 500,000 customers across the world.[14] Car2Go on the other hand started its service in 2008 with 50 cars in Ulm. They provide only one product—'smart fortwo' cars with either combustion or electronic engines. The business model is very similar to DriveNow's concept: A typical customer pays a registration fee, as well as a per-minute driving and parking fee.[15] The service is available in the following German cities: Hamburg (700 cars), Düsseldorf/Cologne (600 cars), Berlin (1200 cars), Stuttgart (500 cars), Munich (300 cars), Frankfurt (300 cars).

[9]See DriveNow GmbH & Co. KG (2015).

[10]See Europcar Group (2015).

[11]See Bundesverband CarSharing (2014).

[12]See Car2Go Deutschland GmbH (2015a).

[13]See Bundesverband CarSharing (2015).

[14]See DriveNow GmbH & Co. KG (2015).

[15]See Car2Go Deutschland GmbH (2015b).

Car2Go had over 1 million customers in 8 countries and 30 cities worldwide in 2015.[16]

2.2.2 Bike Sharing

Since its introduction, bike sharing has not stagnated and has managed to establish a relevant position in the sharing economy market. For example in October 2015, the Münchner Verkehrsgesellschaft mbH introduced a fleet of 1200 bikes across the inner city of Munich.[17] However, the biggest bike sharing provider in Germany for 2015 was Call a Bike belonging to the DB Rent GmbH and the Deutsche Bahn Group. The pricing model (Fig. 9) includes a subscription model where the user pays on a monthly (9 € per month) or yearly (49 € per year) basis and is allowed to use a bike for free within the first 30 min each day.[18] Afterwards the service costs 1 € per 30 min and is capped at 15 € per day. The service is available in many German cities and had over 700,000 customers in total in 2015.[19]

2.2.3 Scooter Sharing

Even though the German scooter market was still emerging (further details shown in Sect. 2.3), the international market already comprised companies that have been established in the last couple of years (Fig. 10). Scoot Networks Inc., for example, provides a fleet of 400 stationary e-scooters in the area of San Francisco. Two different price plans are available for frequent ($19 monthly; $4 per hour) and sporadic ($8 per hour) users. Additionally there is a tourist 2-day pass for $80.[20] Since their foundation in 2012, they have been astonishingly successful in gathering attractive investment partners (in total $4.53 million).[21] Barcelona based Motit by GoingGreen S.L. also uses e-scooters, while the service provider Enjoy by Eni S.p.A. in Milan counts on combustion engines.[22]

2.3 Competitor Analysis

Pascal concurred with Elias that benchmarking of established sharing services is well suited to getting an overview of feasible price plans. At the same time, he kindly advised the task force that the German scooter sharing market and its price structure is essential for comparison with unu's future sharing business model. The task force agreed and additionally researched the main advantages and pain points of existing services (Fig. 11). These could be important factors in outperforming competitors.

[16]See Car2Go Deutschland GmbH (2015c).

[17]See Münchner Verkehrsgesellschaft mbH (2015).

[18]See Call a Bike Interaktiv (2015).

[19]See MOBIL (2015).

[20]See Scoot Networks (2015).

[21]See Crunch Base (2015).

[22]See Motit World (2015)/See Enjoy (2015).

Three German scooter sharing providers launched their operations in 2015 and were therefore considered as most relevant as a comparison for unu's own e-scooter sharing service. All three providers have in common that they do not manufacture their own scooters, unlike unu. Regarding the driver's license validation, all providers offer an on-site solution as well as an online solution, where customers can show their driver's license via Skype to a customer care agent.

2.3.1 scoo.me

Scoo.me was founded in July 2014 in Munich and began their operations a few months subsequent to a pilot phase. The startup also won funding on the German TV show called 'Höhle der Löwen', which increased its public awareness.[23] The company pursued a quick expansion strategy by stretching their city presence to Munich (50 scooters), Cologne (20 scooters) and Frankfurt (15 scooters). In 2015, the fleet consisted of Vespa and Peugeot scooters. However the vast majority of scooters used conventional combustion engines.[24] In order to cover minimum utilization, the price model is pay per usage (3.60 € per usage and 0.18 € per min after the 30th minute).

2.3.2 eMio

Founded in summer 2015, the Berlin based startup has managed to become the biggest player in the German scooter sharing market in terms of fleet size. The fleet consists of 150 e-scooters made by the manufacturer 'emco' that can last up to 100 km.[25] Instead of using a combustion engine, the e-scooters can be maintained with quick-to-change, portable and light batteries. eMio charges 0.19 € per minute or either 0.59 € per km—whichever is cheaper for the user.[26]

2.3.3 Jaano

Another competitor called Jaano operating in Hamburg had its focus on combustion engines. Regarding fleet size (50 scooters) and price model they lagged behind their competitors (0.19 € per driving minute and 0.11 € per parking minute). Another pain point was the limitation on users: In order to be a member the user needs to be at least 21 years old.[27]

2.4 Customers

In the weeks following the strategy retreat, unu's business development team identified numerous potential customer groups (Fig. 12). Simplified down, all

[23]See Vox (2015) Höhle der Löwen.

[24]See Scoo.me Smartphone App (2015).

[25]See emco e-Scooter (2015).

[26]See eMio Sharing (2015).

[27]See Jaano (2015).

potential customers could be divided into two different segments according to their consumer behavior: On the one hand, the group of frequent users, for example, students or commuters, who use the scooters more or less regularly for their way to work/home/university or for other inner city rides. On the other hand, the sporadic users, who are not really interested in frequent use of the scooters because they normally use the public transport, cars or because they are only in town for a few days. One group within this second segment would be tourists, who only spend a couple of days within the city and who do not have their own car or bike with them.

In unu's eyes the more important and more promising segment were the frequent users and in particular within this segment, students. This special group is normally profoundly mobile, open to new experiences and permanently short of money, which also means that most of them cannot afford to own a car. Therefore, the most important fact for them besides a high availability of scooters would be the price of using unu's scooters.

Another possible way of clustering potential customers would be according to their willingness to pay. However, more important than the choice of segmentation method in general was not only to concentrate on a specific group of customers, but to try to integrate all kinds of users: Any customer is a good customer.

2.5 Cost Structure and Cash Requirements

Besides conducting a first customer analysis, unu's finance team also started to make a first feasibility study. To have a certain starting point for their calculations, unu assumed a launch for their new business with 200 scooters in 2016, thereafter increasing that number by another 100 scooters in 2017.

In addition, unu expected to have different kinds of synergies, which, however, have not yet been enumerated. The danger of cannibalization effects for unu's core business due to the fact that people could simply use scooter sharing instead, was also raised during the feasibility study. However, unu decided not to consider that effect in their feasibility study because other synergies are expected to outweigh the negative potential. Furthermore, unu's scooter customers do not come exclusively from a city where sharing would be offered, but from many different German cities.

Regarding the cost side of the new business model, the finance team identified five different key cost categories: Staff, marketing, administration, and IT, as well as cost for scooters (incl. maintenance).

The expenditures for staff included a chief technology officer, an accountant, a motor mechanic, two runners as well as two customer care employees. During the first year, there was also planned a certain budget for IT developers and designers (purpose: development of IT infrastructure and smartphone-app). All salaries were calculated in line with German sectoral averages. Included under IT were continuous costs for telecommunication and IT infrastructure, such as homepage, servers, app maintenance, telephone, internet, computers, software, etc., whereas office equipment (one-time and continuous), rent for office and storing room as well as legal fees and insurances (incl. scooter insurance) were included in administration costs.

To ensure a quick and successful market entry, the marketing budget was planned to include all-year advertising posters as well as a year-long Facebook advertising campaign. Facebook advertising was in Pascal's eyes a perfect way to target the very important student customer group.

The most important cost category, although not the biggest, was expected to be the scooters (incl. maintenance). This category included all kinds of cost which occur during a scooter's lifetime. The cost of scooter (battery) acquisition was depreciated over 3 years (2 years). All other initial costs like helmets or conversion were entered immediately. A summary of the scooter lifetime costs is given in the Fig. 13.

unu expected the distribution of cost categories to change over time, starting with relatively high costs for staff (due to the cost of developers) changing to increasingly high costs for scooters (incl. maintenance). The detailed distribution of costs for the years 2016 and 2019 can be found in Fig. 14.

After summing up all different cost categories, the total expected cost for unu in 2016 (2017) was calculated at 381,851 € (286,436 €) in the first half and 313,220 € (285,066 €) in the second half. These costs included all depreciations, staff costs and other costs according to P&L and balance sheet regulations. For 2018, the total costs were estimated at around 583,024 € and 647,672 € for 2019. The expected increase of cost in the years 2018 and 2019 resulted from the replacement of the first parts of the battery inventory in 2018 and parts of the scooter fleet in 2019. More details on the distribution of costs to the different categories in the different years and about necessary replacement investments can be found in the Fig. 15.

Pascal and Elias were somewhat overwhelmed by all the numbers and therefore asked their finance team to inform them only of the amount of money they would need to invest to launch e-scooter sharing as an expansion of unu's core business. After further consideration, the finance team came to the conclusion that 580,000 € cash would be required in 2016 (Fig. 16), which included a finance buffer of 275,000 € and the necessary initial investment in 200 scooters and 300 additional batteries (both in total 305,000 €). All other costs should be covered during the year by the net sales of the scooter business. For 2017, the finance team expected the necessary cash required to be up to 157,000 € for the increase of the scooter fleet and battery inventory by another 100 e-scooters and 250 additional batteries. These necessary and planned investments should be covered as far as possible by the free cash-flows of the scooter business itself. However, it was deemed unlikely that all costs could be covered without considering synergy effects.

It was Pascal and Elias' wish that the running costs at least would be covered by net sales.

2.6 Target Cities

After taking several databases into account,[28] six major German cities remained for further analysis. Elias and Pascal informed the task force that one city should be chosen for a pilot project due to financial risk and resources for planning. However, the team was also tasked with identifying potential cities for future expansions in advance. This would be essential and might convince investors by showing the growth potential and sustainability of the business model. Elias added that scalability is one of the most important considerations and therefore proposed developing clusters and weighting the following criteria differently: (1) population, (2) share of students as an important customer group, availability of mobility solutions such as (3) public transport, (4) car- and (5) bike-sharing services, (6) fine dust pollution and (7) grade of congestion. Since unu originated in Munich and moved to Berlin this year, the strategic value of unu's headquarters is an important criterion and its impact should not be undervalued when seeking a target city (Fig. 17).

3 Executive Summary

Elias was very optimistic and loved the idea of e-scooter sharing. He was sure that the team was capable of grasping the opportunity. The idea was in line with current mega trends and targeted new potential customers. Other sharing concepts have shown steep growth in recent years. More and more customers are using at least one of these mobility solutions. He came to the conclusion that if car sharing and bike sharing work that well, scooter sharing could also be a success story. unu is an innovative startup which aims to improve mobility solutions for people living in a city. unu as a company was ideally suited to expanding into this type of business. He also thought that they could raise the required cash of 580,000 € to finance the pilot project, either on their own or with an investor. Pascal had some concerns about the required revenue. He wanted to know how the pricing model would look and how many customers were needed to achieve break-even within the first few years. If it appeared to be a profitable business, he also was in favor of the idea, and would want a recommendation from his business development team about a suitable target city for launching the pilot project.

4 Case Questions

Is e-scooter sharing a prosperous second strand to complement unu's existing business model? What would you recommend to Elias and Pascal, after answering the following questions?

[28]See Statistisches Bundesamt (2014)/See Inrix (2015)/See Urban Rail (2015)/See Umweltbundesamt (2015).

- Develop an easy and suitable pricing model for the e-scooter sharing.
- Think of potential synergy effects for unu.
- Give a first insight into how many customers are needed to achieve break-even within the first year of operation.
- Identify appropriate target cities for unu's e-scooter sharing. Make a recommendation on where to launch the pilot project and potentially recommend two further cities for expansion.
- Identify potential opportunities as well as risks. Does the new business model fit to unu's strategic scope? Explain why it may or may not fit.
- A look into the future: Think of some strategic steps for the future to expand utilization of the scooters and to increase revenues.

5 Appendix

5.1 Appendix: Case Description

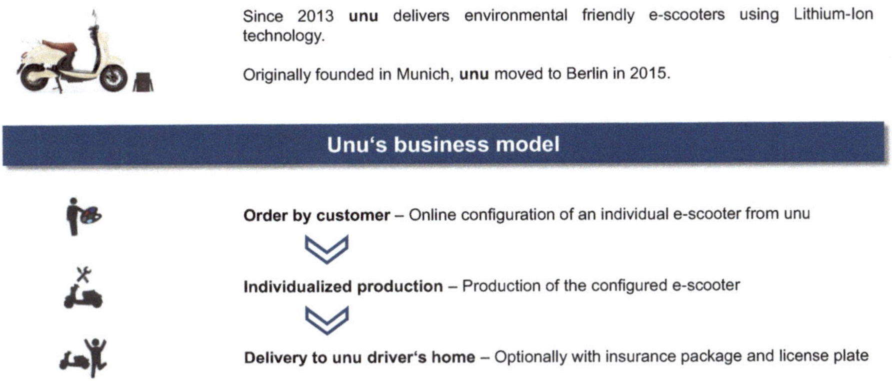

Fig. 1 unu's business model [Own illustration using information from unu GmbH (2015a)]. Source: www.unumotors.com

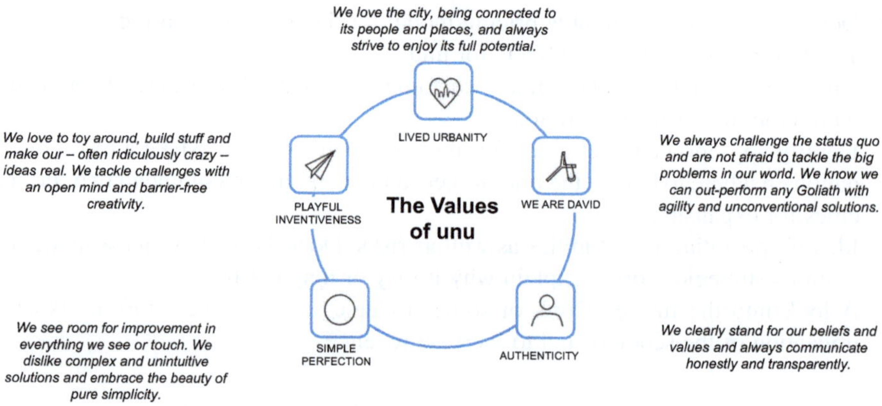

Fig. 2 unu's values [Own illustration using information from unu GmbH (2015a)]. Source: www.unumotors.com

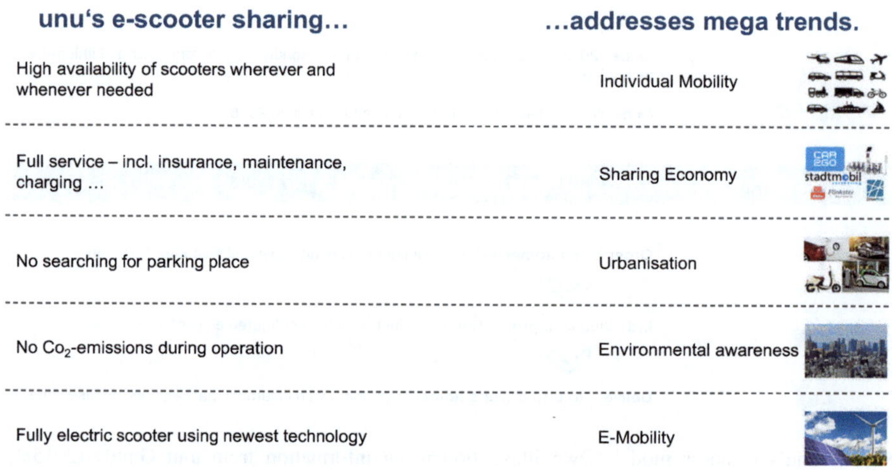

Fig. 3 unu's e-scooter sharing addressing mega trends (Own illustration based on own work). Sources: www.stadtmobil.de, www.clipartlogo.com, www.cdn2.itpro.co.uk, www.fleetwoner.com, www.bmw.com, www.cpp.edu, www.i.auto-bild.de, www.carsharingduesseldorf.com, www.mannheim.de, www.easycarsharing.de, www.carsharing4you.de, www.blogs-images.forbes.com

unu's e-scooter sharing...	**...addresses customers' needs.**
High availability of scooters wherever and whenever needed	Flexibility (time, ways,...)
Full service – incl. insurance, maintenance, charging ...	Affordable and carefree mobility
No searching for parking place	No need for dedicated parking spaces
No Co_2-emissions during operation	Environmentally friendly mobility
Fully electric scooter using newest technology	Support of new technologies

Key drivers for successful launch are **adequate pricing** and **a sufficient number of scooters**.

Fig. 4 unu's e-scooter sharing addressing customers' needs (Own illustration based on own work)

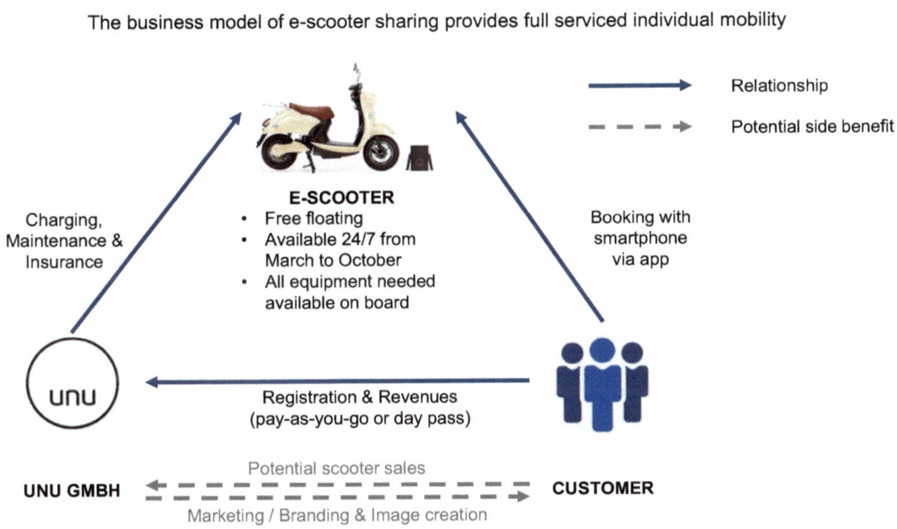

Fig. 5 Business model of e-scooter sharing (Own illustration based on own work). Sources: www.unumotors.com, www.ideengarage.org, www.handelspromotion.de

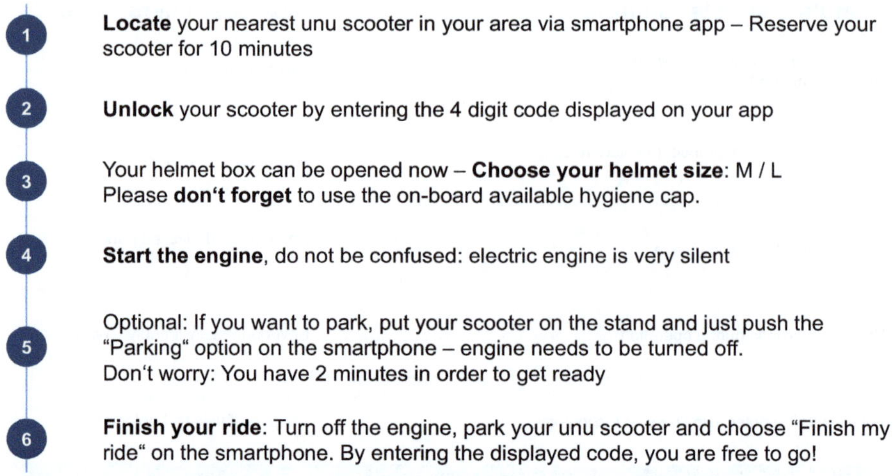

Fig. 6 Booking process (Own illustration based on own work)

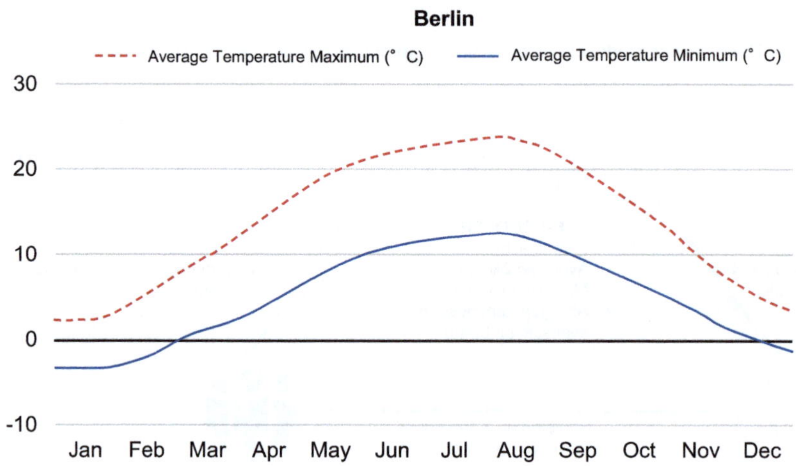

Fig. 7 Climate diagram of Berlin [Source: www.wetter.de (2015)]

Car sharing in Germany has gained a lot of importance since 1997:

Not only has the **amount of vehicles** for car sharing (**2015: > 15,000 vehicles**) gone up, also the **number of people** using them (**2015: > 900,000 people**) has strongly increased.

How did DriveNow and Car2Go start?

DriveNow
- In Berlin
- In 2011
- With 250 cars
- Operation area of 90km²
- 30,000 customers within the first 15 months

CAR 2GO
- In Ulm
- In 2008
- With 50 cars
- 20,000 customers within short time

Fig. 8 Facts on car sharing in Germany [Own illustration using information from Bundesverband Carsharing (2015)/Carsharing-experten (2015)/DriveNow (2012)]. Sources: www.carsharingduesseldorf.com, www.easycarsharing.de, www.carsharing.de

Car Sharing	Primary Plan	Registration Fee	Free Min	€ / time	€ / parking Min
DriveNow	€ / min € / h	19 €	30 min	0.34 € / min	0.15 €
Car2Go	€ / min € / h	19 €	-	0.29 € / min	0.19 €
Flinkster	€ / year & hour	120 € / year	-	2.25 € / h	0.00 €
Bike Sharing	**Primary Plan**	**Monthly / Yearly Fee**	**Free Min**	**€ after 30th min**	**Daily Cap**
Call-a-bike (Regular users)	€ / month € / year	9 € / month 49 € / year	30 min / use 30 min / use	2 € / h 2 € / h	12 € / day 12 € / day
MVG (Regular users)	€ / min € / year	0.08 € / min 48 € / year	- 30 min / use	0.08 € 0.05 €	

Fig. 9 Price structures of some sharing providers [Own illustration using information from DriveNow (2015a)/Car2Go (2015a)/Flinkster (2015)/Callabike (2015)/Münchner Verkehrsgesellschaft (2015)]

Fig. 10 Scooter sharing international and national [Own illustration using information from Scoot (2015)/Motit (2015)/Enjoy (2015)/Emio (2015)/Jaano (2015)/Scoo.me (2015)]. Sources: www.emio-sharing.de, www.scoo.me, www.jaano.de, www.scootnetworks.com, www.motitworld.com, www.enjoy.eni.com

	Primary Plan	Reg. Fee	Free Min	€ / use	€ / min	€ / km	€ / parking min
eMio	€ / min € / km	14 € / 19 €	25 / 100	0.00 €	0.19 €	0.59 €	0.05 €
Scoo.me	€ / usage	0.00 €	0	3.60 €	0.18 € (after 30 min)	0.00 €	0.07 €
Jaano	€ / min	19.90 €	25	0.00 €	0.00 €	0.00 €	0.11 €

(1) Scenario 1: Only driving, no parking – Example: One-Way Use
eMio & Jaano are cheaper within the first 19 minutes, then scoo.me is cheaper

(2) Scenario 2: Driving & parking (50:50) – Example: 15 min driving, 30 min parking, 15 min driving:
- until 19th minute: **eMio & Jaano are cheapest**
- **eMio** beats **Jaano** due to parking costs by far

Fig. 11 Pricing models of scooter sharing providers [Own illustration using information from Emio (2015)/Scoo.me (2015)/Jaano (2015)]

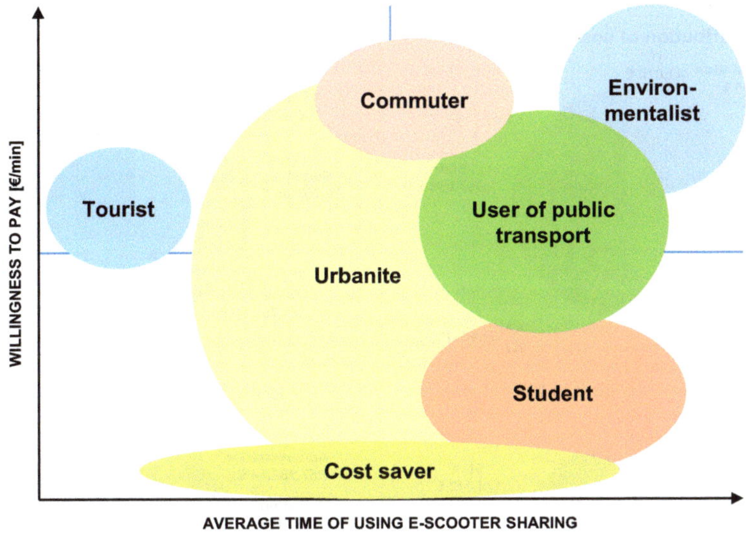

Fig. 12 Customer groups (Own illustration based on own work)

Cost	Amount	Frequency of occurrence
Cost for scooter acquisition *(incl. one battery)*	1,000.00 €	Once within scooter deduction period
Cost for additional batteries *(1.5 batteries per scooter)*	525.00 €	Once within battery deduction period
Cost for scooter conversion	200.00 €	Once in scooter lifetime
Cost for helmets *(2 helmets per scooter)*	100.00 €	Once in scooter lifetime
Cost for scooter depreciation	216.67 €	Per year and scooter
Cost for battery depreciation	175.00 €	Per year and battery
Cost for scooter maintenance	50.00 €	Per year and scooter

Fig. 13 E-scooter sharing—Lifetime costs of e-scooter (Own illustration based on own work)

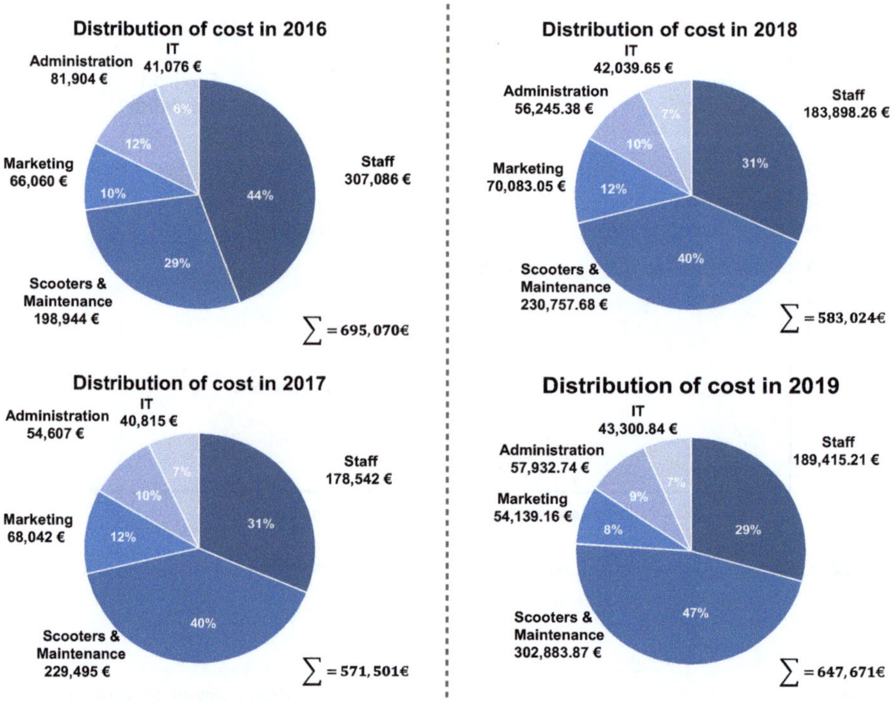

Fig. 14 E-scooter sharing—Distribution of Costs in 2016–2019 (Own illustration based on own work)

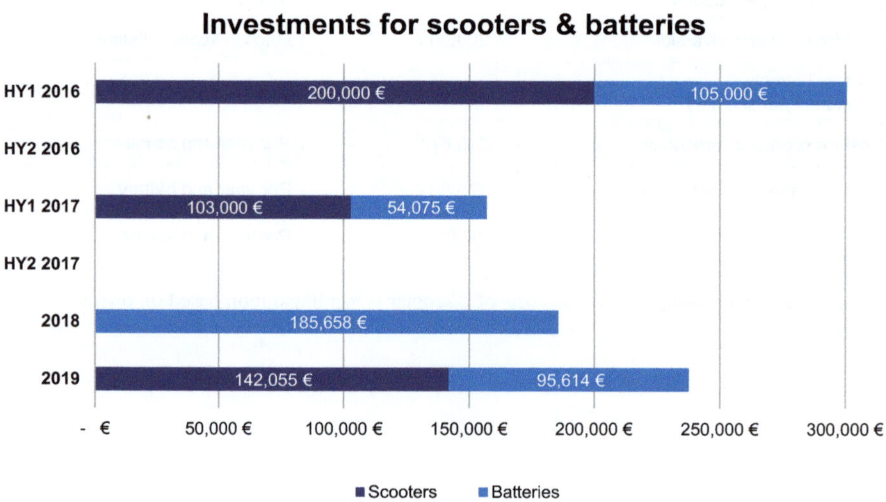

Fig. 15 E-scooter sharing—Investments (Own illustration based on own work)

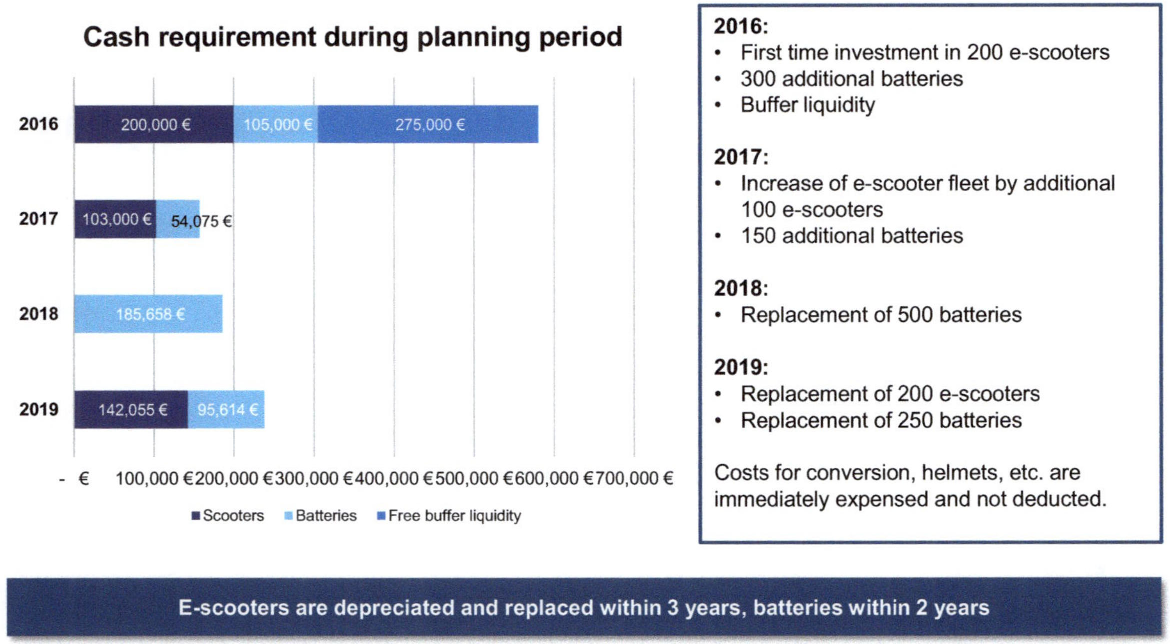

Fig. 16 Overview of necessary (re-) investments and cash in 2016–2019 (Own illustration based on own work)

Criteria	Berlin	Hamburg	Munich	Cologne	Stuttgart	Düsseldorf
Population	3,421,829	1,746,234	1,407,836	1,034,175	604,297	598,686
% Students (of population)	4.37%	5.26%	9.06%	8.96%	14.18%	6.77%
Public Transport	U, S, Tram	U, S	U, S, Tram	LR	S, LR	S, LR, Tram
Car sharing (cars/1000inh.)	0.85	0.84	0.98	1.15	1.44	0.96
Bike sharing (bikes/1000inh.)	0.57	0.94	1.74	1.74	0.66	0.67
Scooter Sharing (number)	150	50	35	15	-	-
Fine dust ($\mu g/m^3$)	32	29	27	29	38	25
Congestion (h/a)	23	48	48	65	64	58
Synergies UNU	Actual seat	-	Foundation	-	-	-

U = Metro; S = S-Bahn in city; LR = Lightrail

Fig. 17 Facts on distinct German cities [Own illustration using information from Statistisches Bundesamt (2014)/Wikipedia (2015)/Inrix (2015)/Prinz Redaktion (2015)/Landeshauptstadt Stuttgart (2015)/Kölner Verkehrs-Betriebe AG (2015)/Nextbike (2015)/Deutsche Bahn AG (2015)/Urbanrail.net (2015)/Bundesverband Carsharing (2015)/Umweltbundesamt (2015)/ MOBIL in Deutschland e.V. (2013)]

5.2 Appendix: Case Solution

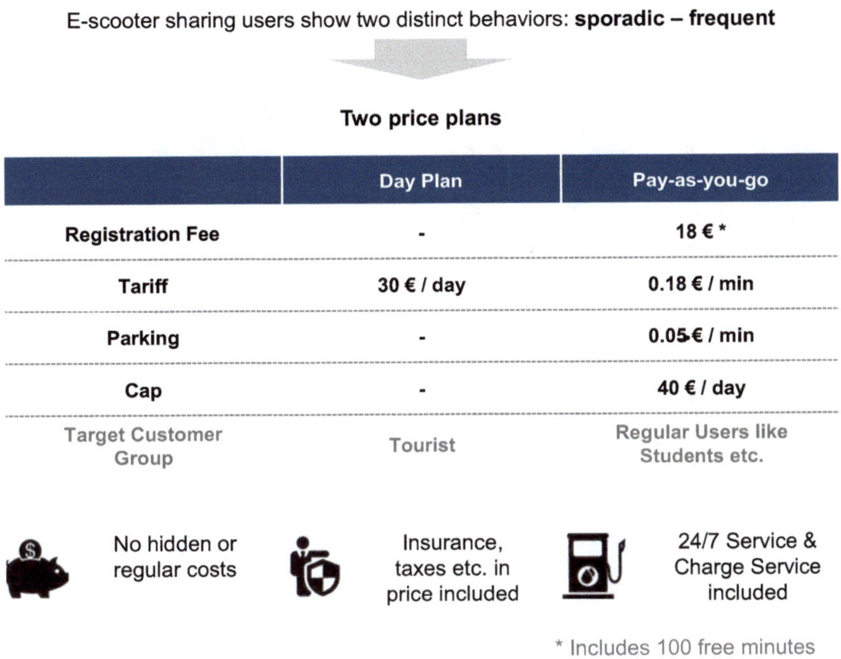

	Day Plan	Pay-as-you-go
Registration Fee	-	18 € *
Tariff	30 € / day	0.18 € / min
Parking	-	0.05€ / min
Cap	-	40 € / day
Target Customer Group	Tourist	Regular Users like Students etc.

Fig. 18 E-scooter sharing—Price model (Illustration based on own work)

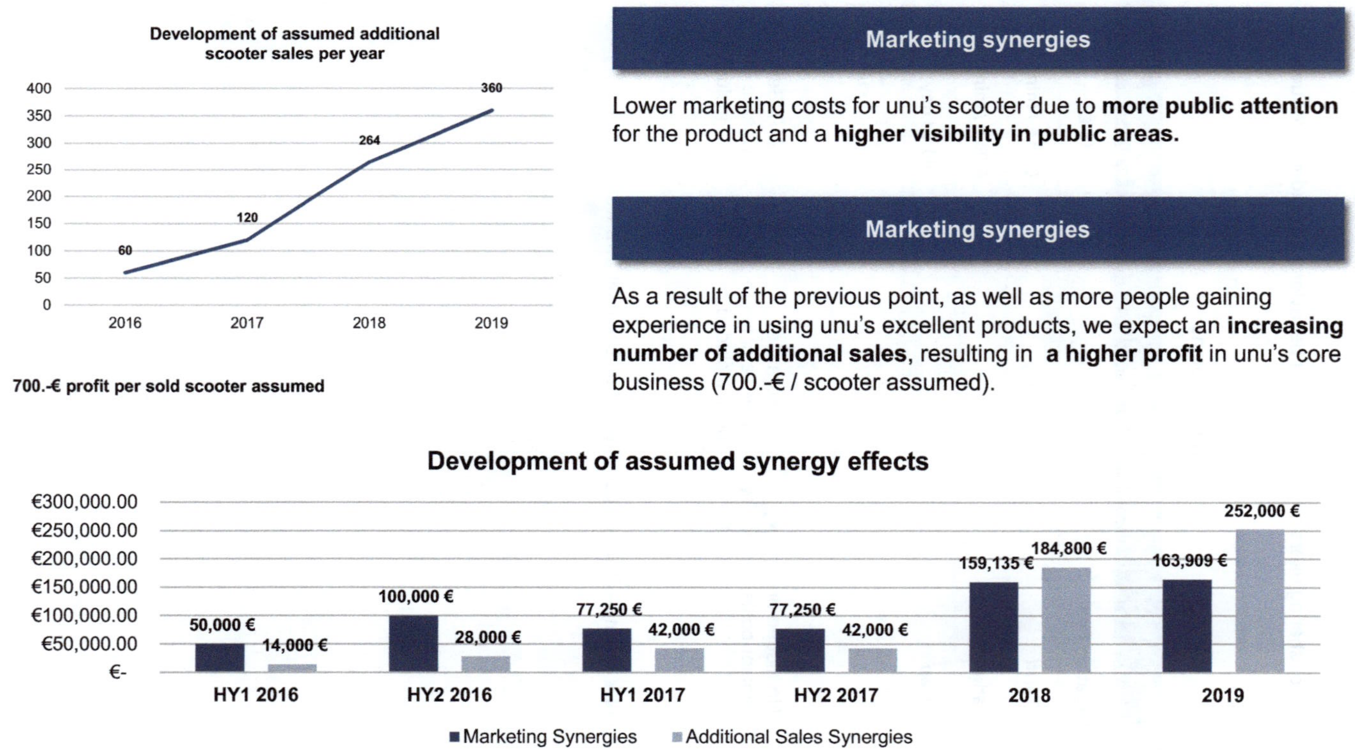

Fig. 19 E-scooter sharing—Synergy effects (Illustration based on own work)

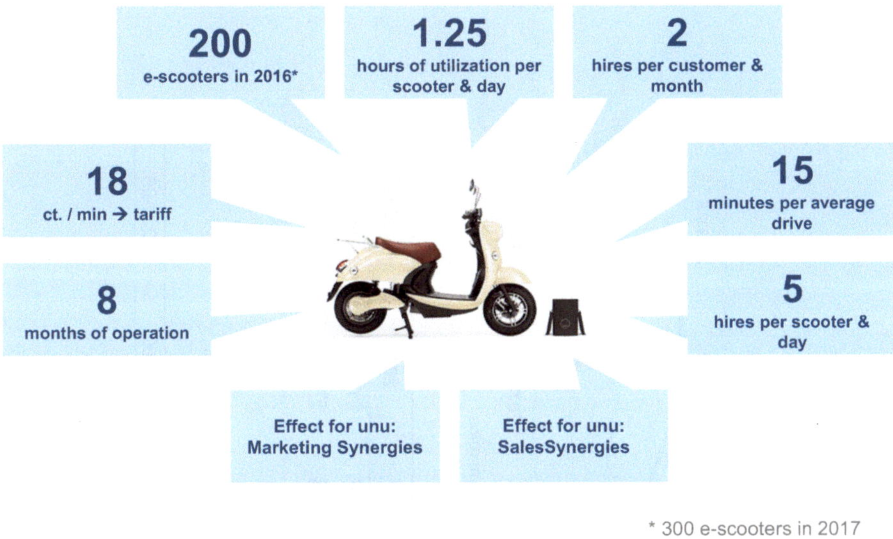

Fig. 20 Key assumptions (Own illustration based on own work). Source: www.unumotors.com

Berlin

	Average usage *	Revenues *	Registrated Customers	Number of cars
DriveNow	78 min / day	24 € per car and day	160,000	1,050
Car2Go	62 min / day	18 € per car and day	95,000	1,200
Multicity	26 min / day	7 € per car and day	10,000	350

Berlin, Hamburg, Munich, Cologne and Düsseldorf

	Average usage *	Revenues *
DriveNow	58 min / day	18 € per car and day
Car2Go	54 min / day	16 € per car and day

Worldwide

	Registrated Customers	Number of cars	Places of operation
DriveNow	500,000	3,800	9
Car2Go	1,000,000	13,000	30

Data has not been confirmed by the car sharing companies

Fig. 21 Study of Civity (2014)—Facts on car sharing in Germany [Own illustration using information from Wirtschaftswoche (2014)/Car2Go (2015a)/DriveNow (2015a)]

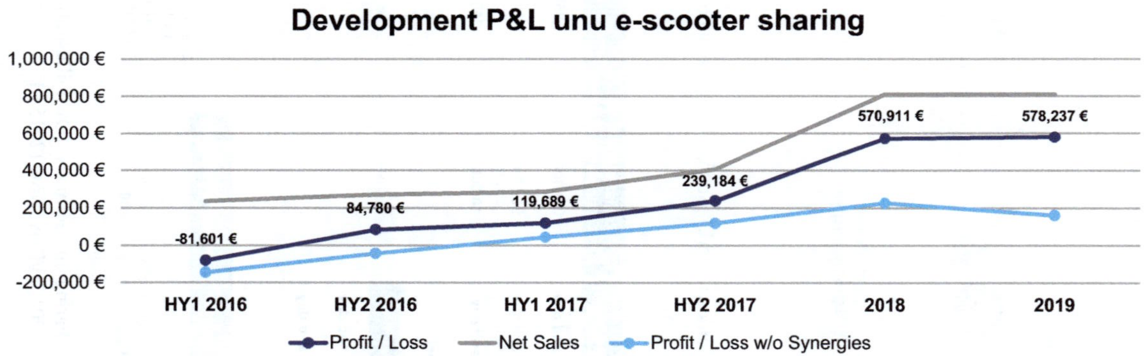

	HY1 2016	HY2 2016	HY1 2017	HY2 2017	2018	2019
Net Sales	236,250 €	270,000 €	286,875 €	405,000 €	810,000 €	810,000 €
Profit / Loss	**-81,601€**	**84,780 €**	**119,689 €**	**239,184 €**	**570,911 €**	**578,237 €**
Profit / Loss w/o Synergies	-145,601 €	-43,220 €	439 €	119,934 €	226,976 €	162,328 €
Total Synergies	64,000 €	128,000 €	119,250 €	119,250 €	343,935 €	415,909 €
Total Cost	381,851 €	313,220 €	286,436 €	285,066 €	583,024 €	647,672 €
No. of Customers	13,125	15,000	15,938	22,500	22,500	22,500

Fig. 22 E-scooter sharing—Development P&L (Own illustration based on own work)

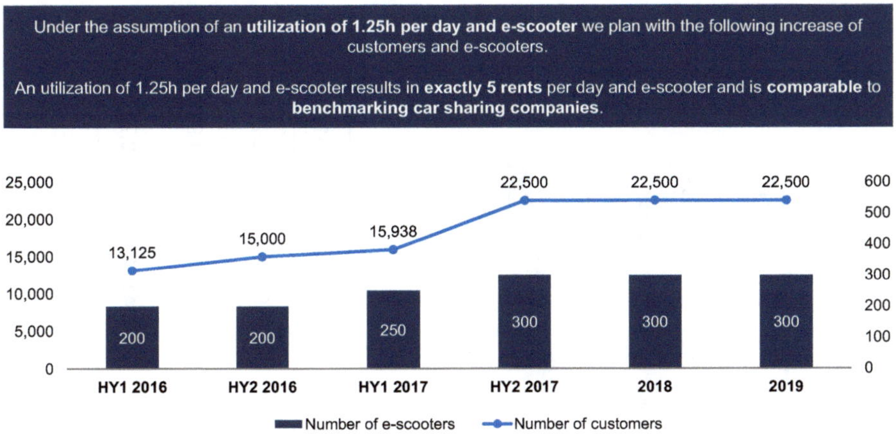

Fig. 23 Development of number of customers and e-scooters (Own illustration based on own work)

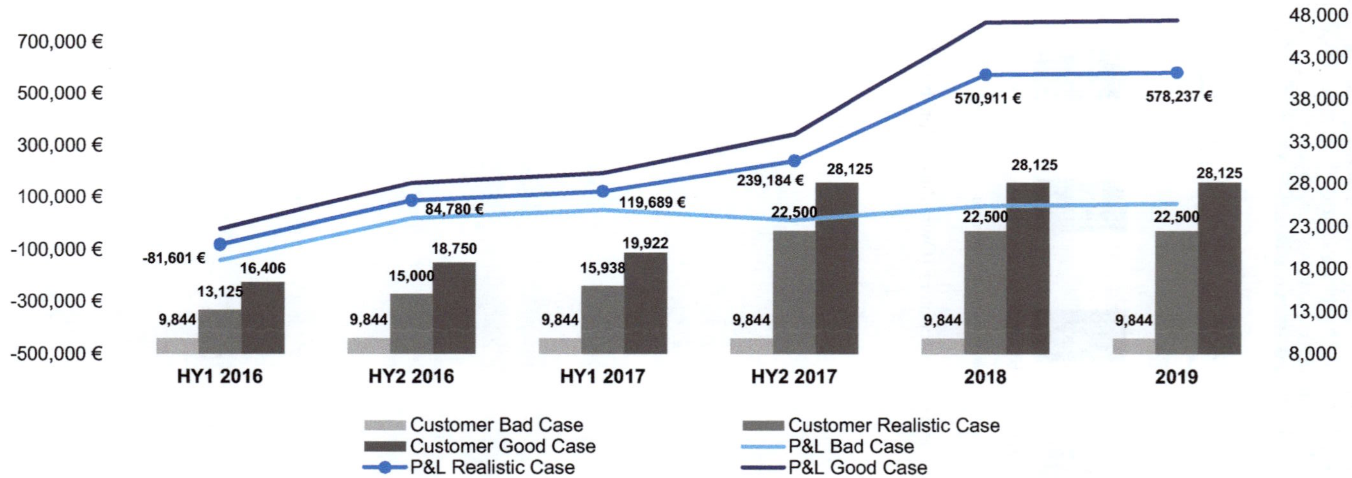

	HY1 2016	HY2 2016	HY1 2017	HY2 2017	2018	2019
P&L Realistic Case *100% of Customers*	- 81,601 €	84,780 €	119,689 €	239,184 €	570,911 €	578,237 €
P&L Bad Case *75% of Customers*	- 140,663 €	17,280 €	47,970 €	11,372 €	64,661 €	71,987 €
P&L Good Case *125% of Customers*	- 22,538 €	152,280 €	191,408 €	340,434 €	773,411 €	780,737 €

Fig. 24 Sensitivity analysis (Own illustration based on own work)

Criteria	Berlin	Hamburg	Munich	Cologne	Stuttgart	Düsseldorf	Weight
Population	6	5	4	3	2	1	10
% Students	1	2	5	4	6	3	15
Public Transport	6	4	6	3	4	6	15
Car sharing	2	1	4	5	6	3	10
Bike sharing	6	3	2	1	5	4	20
Scooter Sharing	1	2	2	4	6	6	10
Fine dust	5	3	2	4	6	1	10
Congestion	2	3	3	6	5	4	5
Synergies UNU	6	1	4	1	1	1	20
TOTAL	**495**	**295**	**420**	**335**	**495**	**365**	**115**

Fig. 25 Target cities—Evaluation matrix (Own illustration based on own work)

unu vs. eMio

Category	unu	eMio	Winner
Price	18 ct. / min	19 ct. / min	unu
Registration fee	18 €	19 €	unu
Number of scooters	200 / 300 scooters	150 scooters	unu
Scooter supply	internal	External	unu
Start of operation	March 2016	June 2015	eMio
Engine type	Electric		No winner
Quality & service	Unu offers a higher product quality and has better knowledge about scooters		unu

Anyway we expect that customers will use both service providers, co-existence should be possible.

Fig. 26 unu vs. eMio [Own illustration based on own work and emio (2015)]. Sources: www.unumotors.com, www.emio-sharing.de

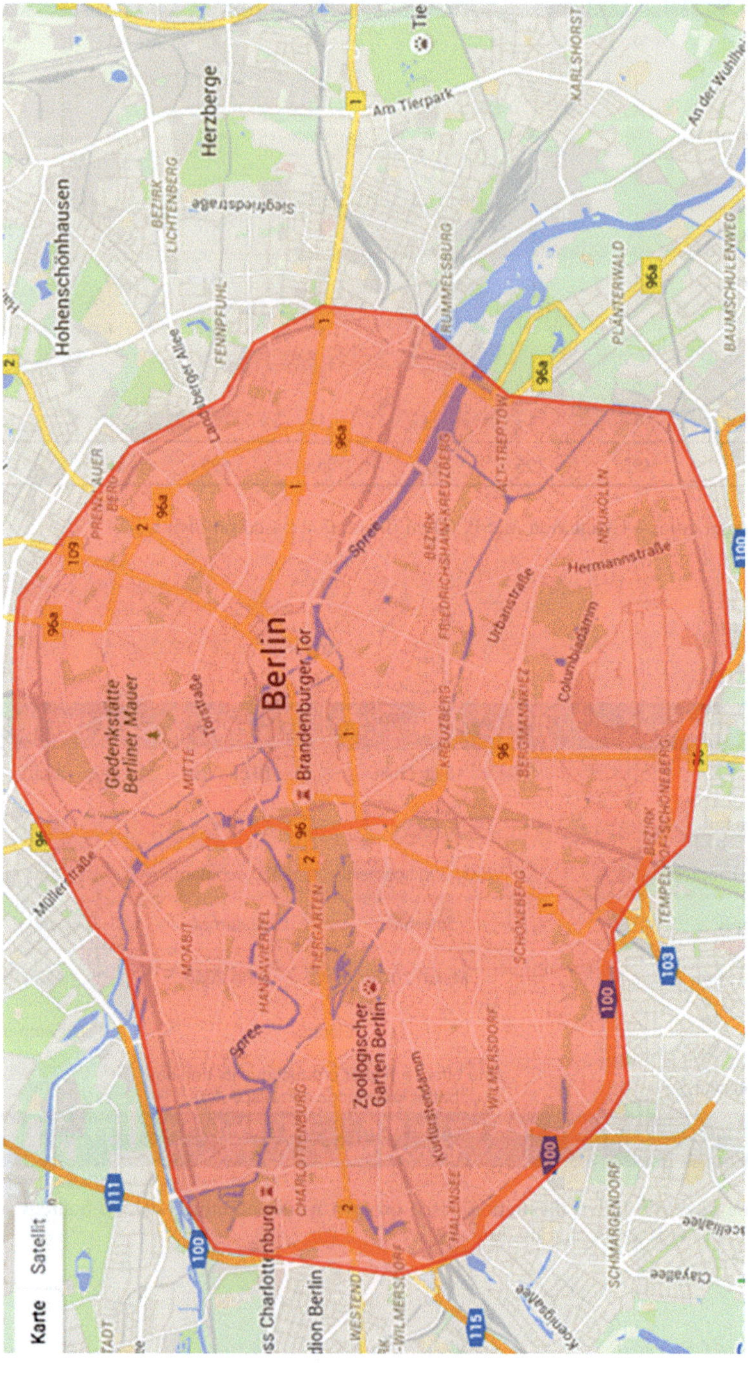

Fig. 27 E-scooter sharing—Operation area in Berlin (Own illustration based on own work). Source: www.google.de/maps/place/Berlin/

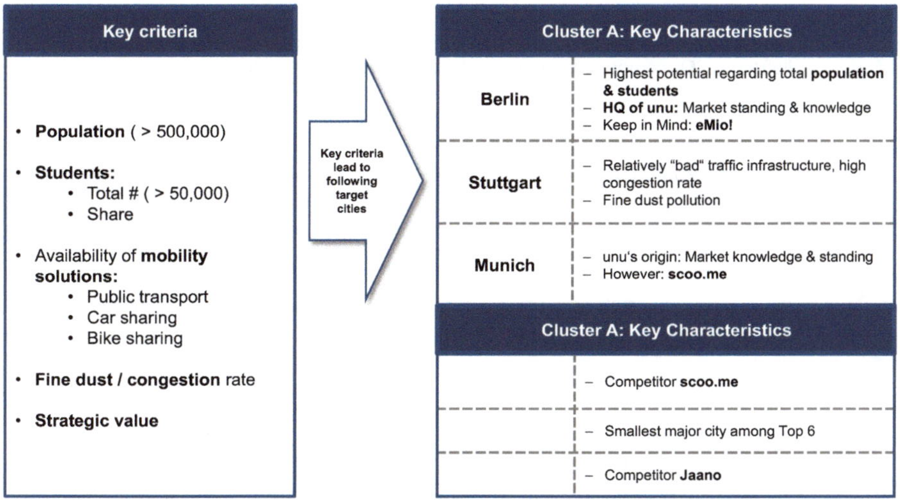

Fig. 28 Potential target cities for e-scooter sharing (Own illustration based on own work)

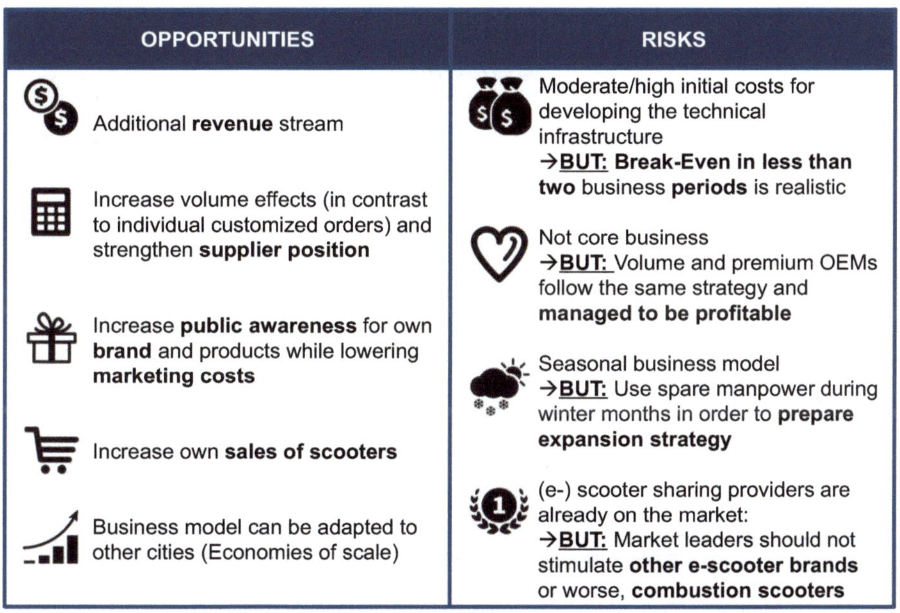

Fig. 29 Risks and opportunities (Own illustration based on own work)

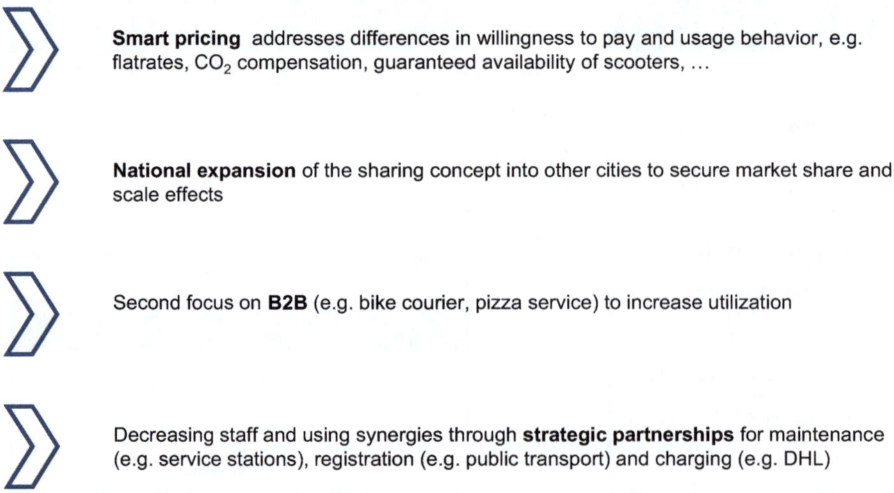

Fig. 30 Further steps—Overview (Own illustration based on own work)

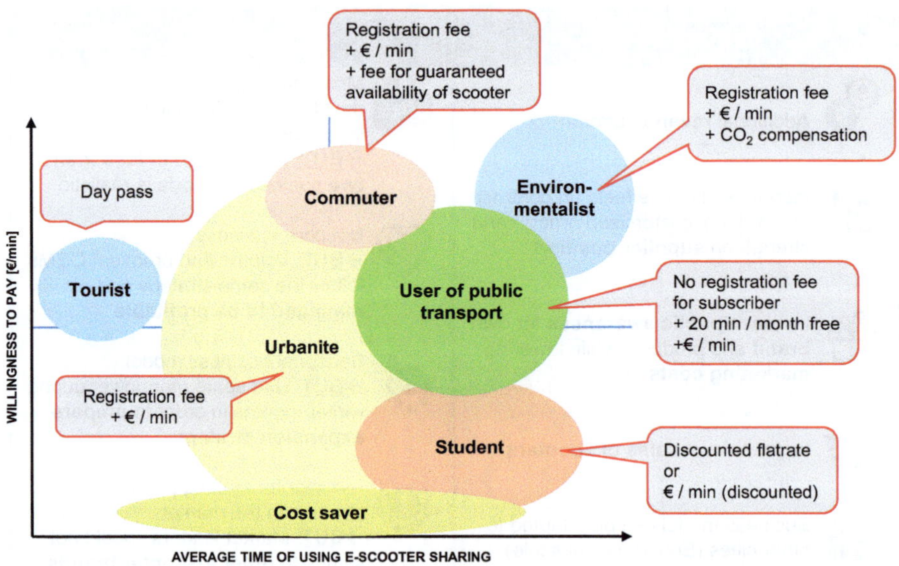

Fig. 31 Smart pricing (Own illustration based on own work)

Service stations
Maintenance and reparations operated by a partner service station
→ **Benefit:** No staff for maintenance needed
→ **Benefit:** No room for service station needed

VBB MVV VVS

Public transport
User can register for sharing at any selling point of public transport
→ **Benefit:** No staff for registration needed

DHL
5-10 charging stations per packing station
1. User gets mTan (mobile transaction number) for opening one door of the packing station
2. User changes empty into full battery

→ **Benefit:** Less staff for charging required

Fig. 32 Strategic partnerships (Own illustration based on own work). Source: www.scooter-werkstatt-koblenz.de, www.vbb.de, www.mentzdv.de, www.livinglab-bwe.de, www.heise.de

6 Case Solution

6.1 Pricing Model

The business development team proposed keeping the pricing structure as simple as possible so that customers could easily and quickly understand the tariffs. To begin with, two tariffs should be taken into account to address the frequent usage behaviors on the one hand and the sporadic usage behaviors on the other hand (Fig. 18).

Frequent users (e.g. students, commuters) would get the opportunity to use a pay-as-you-go tariff. This price plan includes a one-time registration fee of 18.00 € for 100 free minutes of e-scooter use, a tariff of 0.18 € per minute for driving, and a tariff of 0.05 € per minute for parking. The tariff is limited to 40.00 € per day to cap the potential costs for the users.

A day plan of 30 € per day would be offered to sporadic users (e.g. tourists). The day plan allows the customers to use all available scooters during the booked day, parking costs not included. This tariff does not require an extra fee for registration, keeping it attractive for one-time users.

The prices were gross, already including insurances, taxes, 24/7 service and charging service, guaranteeing the customers that there are no regular or hidden costs. Potential customers want affordable pricing. Compared to competitors, the tariffs are cheaper and about half the price of car sharing providers.

6.2 Synergy Effects

During the financial analysis, unu's finance and business development team identified two major synergy effects for unu's core business (Fig. 19). First, unu's e-scooter sharing would help to increase public awareness of unu's products, because at least 200 scooters would be available around the city. This provides perfect additional advertising as it allows potential buyers the possibility of experiencing the product straight away. The team expected that this additional public awareness would result in a lower need for marketing expenditures for unu's core business.

Second, and as a result of the first synergy effect, the team anticipated a strong increase in scooter sales after launching the e-scooter sharing as a result of the additional marketing and the already mentioned possibility of trying out the product without having to arrange a test drive. With more people enjoying driving unu's e-scooters, more people were expected to buy themselves their own scooter. This could especially apply to people who do not live in one of unu's target cities, but were impressed by the unu scooter experience.

These additional sales of unu scooters due to increased awareness and familiarity with the product were valued at 700 € per scooter and included by the team in the finance calculations as along with the other specific assumptions.

6.3 Number of Customers for Break-Even

In order to calculate the specific number of customers required to reach the financial break-even point, unu made specific assumptions (Fig. 20): in line with the average usage of different German car sharing companies (Fig. 21), unu expected that the average utilization per scooter per day would be 1.25 h. Additionally, it was expected that the average sharing customer would use the e-scooters on average twice a month for 15 min.[29] This yields five hires per scooter per day (1.25 h, equaling 75 min divided by 15 min).

As outlined in Sect. 6.2, synergy effects had to be included in the calculations, resulting in a total of 192,000 € in the first year.

To achieve the break-even point during the first year, all costs in 2016 would have to be covered by net sales. The total cost for the first year was calculated at 695,071 €. After deducting the expected synergy effects of 192,000 €, the cost to be covered by net sales was 503,071 € (Figs. 22, 23 and 24).

According to these assumptions, an average user spends two times 2.70 € per month (0.18 € per minute multiplied by 15 min), resulting in a user-specific net sale [after deduction of German sales tax (19%)] of 4.54 € per month. On average, it was expected that unu would operate its sharing business 8 months per year, resulting in annual net sales per customer of 36.32 €.

[29] Average time Germans needed for their way to work in Germany.

As previously mentioned, the remaining total cost after the deduction of expected synergies had to be covered by net sales. unu calculated the following:

$$\textit{Required Average Number of Customers} = \frac{\textit{Total Cost} - \textit{Expected Synergies}}{\textit{Annual Net Sales per Customer}}$$

$$= 13,852 \textit{ Customers}$$

It would be necessary to attract 13,582 customers in the first year of operation. Of course, this represents an average number. Since there would not be sufficient customers from the very first day, the total number of customers would have to be significantly greater at the end of the first year than at the beginning.

6.4 Target Cities

After taking six different cities into consideration, the task force decided that Germany's lively and dynamic capital Berlin would be the best fit for a pilot project, for both economic and strategic reasons (Fig. 25). Berlin has by far the biggest population with 3.4 million citizens and the highest number of students (150,000). Additionally, unu moved its headquarters to Berlin in March 2015 and therefore gained quite a good knowledge about the market and its potential customers. Furthermore, many people were already aware of unu's market presence and its offerings. Even though its biggest competitor eMio had a pioneer position in Berlin, unu would have advantages regarding the pricing model and its market standing as a manufacturer in both the short and long run (Fig. 26). Therefore, the inner city of Berlin was proposed as the area of operation (Fig. 27). Munich and Stuttgart were regarded as the next best options, which should be chosen for subsequent national expansion (Fig. 28). Munich is interesting for its economic potential and unu's roots offer a strategic advantage. Stuttgart is hampered by relatively bad mobility solutions and a high congestion rate due to its natural topography and its traffic system. The remaining cities of Hamburg, Düsseldorf and Cologne would also be interesting in the long run, but for launching the e-scooter sharing, their downsides outweighed the advantages.

6.5 Risks and Opportunities

After the team revealed which city to choose, the risks and opportunities were considered as another important factor in evaluating e-scooter sharing (Fig. 29). The most promising opportunity identified is the additional revenue stream. However, the sharing service would not be limited to this factor. Bearing in mind that unu's business model builds upon strongly customized products without a retailer structure, fleets with hundreds of scooters could help achieve volume effects and potentially improve the supplier structure. As unu scooters would be parked across

Berlin, unu would be able to decrease its marketing costs thanks to enhanced public awareness. Additionally, the team expected that people would become familiar with unu's product and potentially purchase an e-scooter, thus leading to further sales. Wrapping up the opportunities, the business model is transferable to cities such as Munich or Stuttgart when taking the city's unique characteristics into account. These economies of scale could enable lower initial costs in implementing the service in another target city.

The risks, on the other hand, were associated with high initial costs for the pilot project, the fact that sharing has not been unu's core business, the seasonality of e-scooter sharing and the pioneer position of other scooter sharing services. Nevertheless, the opportunities far outweighed the risks and could potentially even turn these risks into strengths, e.g. competitive advantage over eMio due to unu's knowledge as a manufacturer, with the possibility to become the number one scooter sharing service in Berlin.

Another relevant question was whether the new sharing concept was in line with unu's existing strategic orientation. Since its foundation the company have pursued partnerships with established companies that have in depth expertise. They have established partnerships with BOSCH-Werkstätten for technical customer support, with LG for the newest and innovative battery technology, and with a manufacturer in China.[30]

These partnerships have enabled unu to grow fast and to be able to react very flexibly to changes. In consideration of this orientation, the proposed scooter sharing concept was in conflict with unu's existing model. On the other hand, arguably, time was running out and therefore unu would be forced to decide whether to join the market or leave it to others. Time for identifying attractive partners and making agreements with would be lacking.

6.6 Outlook for the Future

The task force still felt that they need to convince Elias and Pascal to ensure that they would receive green light for January 2016. Therefore, they presented their findings for future potential (Figs. 30, 31 and 32).

A point neglected within the pilot project was smart pricing. The pricing model should be kept simple to begin with, for technical and invoicing reasons as well as attracting customers. But in the future, people with a higher willingness to pay, such as those motivated by environmental concerns, could be asked to pay a CO_2 premium. Another example would be commuters or business people who want a scooter at a specific location on a specific time during the week or month.

As already mentioned, national expansion was identified as a key for further growth potential.

[30]See unu GmbH (2015d)/See Welt (2014).

The pilot project could also be adapted easily to other cities building upon an already existing technical infrastructure (e.g. smartphone-app, website, invoicing process) and previous experience. Until then, unu could observe how cities with small but existing scooter sharing services in Hamburg, Cologne and Düsseldorf will develop.

With increasing development, unu would also be able to transform its knowledge of the customers' behavior into serious benefits to drastically increase scooter utilization. Beginning with B2C, by observing the driving behavior, spare scooters could be blocked for business customers such as food delivery services. Of course, this B2B model could only be adapted when utilization is very low during downtimes; e.g. 50 of the 300 scooters might be solely available to B2B partners between Mo and Fr. 22:00–07:00.

Strategic partnerships were also regarded as an interesting way of transferring competences such as maintenance, registration and charging to other companies. For example, the process of maintenance could be made leaner with a service station partnership. unu already has a support agreement with BOSCH Service-Partner Werkstätten for its existing business,[31] so a negotiated expansion should be possible. Registration could also be handled by local public sector stations (e.g. MVG ticket offices) in order to decrease the number of customer care agents on its own staff. Last but not least, the charging process could be done in cooperation with parcel stations, e.g. an electrified DHL stationary parcel system where an individual can obtain a fully loaded battery by entering a code.

7 Recommendation

The business development team recommended Elias and Pascal to launch e-scooter sharing as a second branch to complement unu's existing business model. The business model is not only in line with mega trends and addresses customer needs, it also promises important synergy effects for unu's core business of selling scooters. The analysis of potential target cities for e-scooter sharing showed that there are many suitable cities in Germany. Risks were identified, but the business development team shared the opinion that these are manageable. In a nutshell, high profitability could be expected within the first few years.

To launch the pilot project, the business development team recommended Berlin as target city in 2016. First calculations show that on average 13,600 customers would be needed to achieve break-even in 2016. To start with, the pricing model should be kept simple. The business development team suggested a pay-as-you-go tariff of 0.18 € per min for frequent users and a day pass of 30 € per day for sporadic users such as tourists. Before starting, an amount of 580,000 € would be needed to finance the concept for the first year.

[31]See unu GmbH (2015d).

References

Blum, P. (2015). *Feedback of co-founder unu GmbH (w/Pfeiffer, Krauß, Beck, Weidenbach).* Accessed December 17, 2015.

Bundesverband CarSharing. (2014). *CarSharing Entwicklung in Deutschland Parallel.* Accessed December 11, 2015, from http://www.carsharing.de/sites/default/files/uploads/presse/pdf/grafik_entwicklung_carsharing_in_deutschland_2014_parallel.pdf

Bundesverband CarSharing. (2015). *CarSharing Entwickling in Deutschland Gesamt.* Accessed December 11, 2015, from http://www.carsharing.de/sites/default/files/uploads/presse/pdf/grafik_entwicklung_carsharing_in_deutschland_2014_parallel.pdf

Call a Bike Interaktiv. (2015). Accessed December 11, 2015, from https://www.callabike-interaktiv.de/fileadmin/www.callabike-interaktiv.de/redaktion/images/Preissystem_NEU/20150624_Preisverzeichnis_CaB_Final.pdf

Car2Go. (2015a). *car2go: Pionier und Marktführer im vollflexiblen Carsharing.* Accessed December 6, 2015, from https://www.car2go.com/common/data/locations/europe/deutschland/pr_bereich/One_Pager_car2go_August_2015_de.pdf

Car2Go. (2015b). *Tarifordnung gültig ab 08/15.* Accessed December 11, 2015, from https://www.car2go.com/global-tc/de/de-de-prices.pdf

Car2Go. (2015c). *Fact Sheet 08/15.* Accessed December 11, 2015, from https://www.car2go.com/common/data/locations/europe/deutschland/pr_bereich/Fact_Sheet_car2go_August_2015_de.pdf

Carsharing-experten. (2015). *Car2go: Beginn einer Erfolgsgeschichte.* Accessed December 6, 2015, from http://www.carsharing-experten.de/car2go-carsharing/car2go-beginn-einer-erfolgsgeschichte.html/

Crunchbase: *Overview of Scoot Networks – Funding Received.* Accessed December 11, 2015., from https://www.crunchbase.com/organization/scoot-networks

Deutsche Bahn AG (2015) *Call a bike.* Accessed December 1, 2015, from https://www.callabike-interaktiv.de/kundenbuchung/process.php?proc=bikesuche&f=500&&f=500/

DriveNow. (2012). *DriveNow Pressemitteilung: DriveNow mit 30.000 Mitgliedern in Berlin.* Accessed December 6, 2015, from https://de.drive-now.com/fileadmin/application/press/2012-12-13-30000_Mitglieder-in-Berlin.pdf/

DriveNow. (2015). *Factsheet DriveNow.* Accessed December 11, 2015, from https://prod.drive-now-content.com/stage/fileadmin/user_upload_de/12_Presse/Daten_Fakten/DriveNow_Factsheet_September_2015_DE.pdf

emco. (2015). *Classic line: Overview.* Accessed December 11, 2015, from http://www.emco-elektroroller.de/emco-elektroroller-modelle/classic-line/novi-c-1500.html

eMio. (2015). *Preise.* Accessed December 11, 2015, from http://www.emio-sharing.de/#!gebuehren/c9yw

Enjoy. (2015). *Fleet overview in Milan.* Accessed December 11, 2015, from https://enjoy.eni.com/en/milano/flotta

Europcar. (2015). *Corporate profile.* Accessed December 11, 2015, from http://www.europcar-group.com/en/group/corporate-profile/

Flinkster. (2015). *Preisübersicht.* Accessed December 6, 2015, from https://www.flinkster.de/index.php?id=418&f=3/

Inrix. (2015). *Wirtschaftswachstum führt zu mehr Staus in drei Viertel der deutschen Städte.* Accessed December 1, 2015, from http://inrix.com/press/scorecard-report-germany-german/

Jaano. (2015). *FAQ.* Accessed December 11, 2015, from http://jaano.de/faq/

Kölner Verkehrs-Betriebe AG. (2015). *Radfahren Bringts!.* Accessed December 1, 2015, from http://www.kvb-koeln.de/german/fahrplan/fahrradverleih.html/

Landeshauptstadt Stuttgart. (2015). *Call a Bike: Räder und Pedelecs rund um die Uhr.* Accessed December 1, 2015, from https://www.stuttgart.de/callabike/

Mobil. (2015). *Das Magazin der Deutschen Bahn/DB Mobility Logistics AG.* Accessed December 11, 2015.

MOBIL in Deutschland e.V. (2013). *Deutschlands Städtevergleich Automobil 2013*. Accessed December 2, 2015, from http://www.mobil.org/mobil/nachricht/article/deutschlands-staedtevergleich-automobil-2013/

Motit World. (2015). *Frequently asked questions*. Accessed December 11, 2015, from http://www.motitworld.com/eng/faqs

Münchner Verkehrsgesellschaft mbH. (2015). Press release of October 09, 2015, https://www.mvg.de/services/mobile-services/mvg-rad.html

Nextbike. (2015). *Launch of MVG Rad in Munich*. Accessed December 1, 2015, from http://www.nextbike.de/en/news/launch-of-mvg-rad-in-munich/

Prinz Redaktion. (2015). *PRINZ_Test: Car-Sharing und Miet-Fahrräder*. Accessed December 1, 2015, from http://prinz.de/duesseldorf/artikel/101110-prinz-test-car-sharing-und-miet-fahrrader/

Scoo.me. (2015). *Preisliste für München, Köln & Frankfurt*. Accessed December 7, 2015, from https://scoo.me/preisliste.html

Scoot Networks. (2015). *How many scooters are in the fleet*. Accessed December 11, 2015, from http://www.scootnetworks.com/faq/how-many-scoots-are-in-the-fleet/

Statistisches Bundesamt. (2014). *Städte in Deutschland nach Fläche und Bevölkerung auf Grundlage des ZENSUS 2011 und Bevölkerungsdichte*. Gebietsstand: 31.12.2013. Accessed December 1, 2015, from https://www.destatis.de/DE/ZahlenFakten/LaenderRegionen/Regionales/Gemeindeverzeichnis/Administrativ/Aktuell/05Staedte.html/

Umweltbundesamt. (2015). *Jährliche Auswertung Feinstaub*. Accessed December 2, 2015, from https://www.umweltbundesamt.de/search/content/feinstaub/

unu GmbH. (2015a). *About us*. Accessed December 6, 2015, from https://unumotors.com/de/about-us/

unu GmbH. (2015b). *Charging unu*. Accessed January 4, 2015, from https://unumotors.com/de/product/charging-unu

unu GmbH. (2015c). *Business model*. Accessed December 6, 2015, from https://unumotors.com/de/business-model

unu GmbH. (2015d). *Support*. Accessed January 3, 2015, from https://unumotors.com/de/support

Urbanrail.net. (2015). *UrbanRail in Germany*. Accessed December 1, 2015, from http://www.urbanrail.net/eu/de/

Vox. (2015). *Kandidaten: Scoo.me*. Accessed December 11, 2015, from http://hoehle-der-loewen.de/kandidaten/scoo-me/

Welt. (2014). http://www.welt.de/regionales/bayern/article132724600/Auf-dem-Roller-lautlos-durch-die-Grossstadt.html

Wikipedia. (2015). *Datenbank – Liste der Hochschulen in Deutschland*. Accessed December 1, 2015, from https://de.wikipedia.org/wiki/Liste_der_Hochschulen_in_Deutschland/

Wirtschaftswoche. (2014). *DriveNow ist erfolgreicher als Car2Go*. Accessed December 6, 2015, from http://www.wiwo.de/unternehmen/auto/carsharing-drivenow-ist-erfolgreicher-als-car2go/10340486.html/

Case: UBS—Acquisition of Commerzbank AG as a Possible Growth Strategy

Fahrudin Abazi, Philipp Deisler, and Michael Eisenlauer

List of Abbreviations

ACR	Asset and Capital Recovery
AG	Aktien gesellschaft
bn	Billion
CAGR	Compound Annual Growth Rate
CEO	Chief Executive Officer
CHF	Swiss franc
CRE	Commercial Real Estate
DAX	Deutscher Aktien index
DDM	Dividend Discount Model
DSB	Deutsche Schiffsbank
EPS	Earnings per Share
EU	European Union or Europe
FAUB	Fachausschuss Unternehmensbewertung und Betriebswirtschaft
FMV	Fair Market Value
FRG	Federal Republic of Germany
FSMA	Agency for Financial Market Stabilization
GDP	Gross Domestic Product
HSBC	Hongkong and Shanghai Banking Corporation Holdings (Bank)
IRR	Internal Rate of Return
IT	Information Technology
m	Million
MCAP	Market Capitalization

Submitted by: Fahrudin Abazi, Philipp Deisler, Michael Eisenlauer
Reviewer: Prof. Dr. Gunther Friedl, Gerald Broneske

F. Abazi (✉) · P. Deisler · M. Eisenlauer
Technical University of Munich, Munich, Germany

G. Friedl, A. Biagosch (eds.), *Case Studies in Strategic Management*, Management for Professionals, https://doi.org/10.1007/978-3-319-95555-1_4

NPV	Net Present Value
p.a.	Per Annum
P/E-Ratio	Price-to-Earnings Ratio
Q&A	Questions and Answers
SS	Sommersemester
TBD	To Be Done
tn	Trillion
TUM	Technische Universität München
UBS	Union de Banques Suisses (Bank)
UK	United Kingdom
US	United States of America
WACC	Weighted Average Cost of Capital

List of Symbols

€	Euro
%	Percent
$	Dollar
&	And

1 Introduction

After four successful years as chairman of the board of directors of UBS and being honored as "European Banker of the Year 2014", Axel Weber was scrutinizing a report he just received. He was examining the new official ranking of the large financial institutes of Europe and the intense look on his face turned gradually into a scowl. According to total assets, the UBS Group AG was not even ranked among the top ten banks in Europe (Fig. 1). Even the fact that UBS Group AG was in fifth place in terms of market capitalization could not lift his mood (Fig. 2). He dropped the stack of papers on his desk, leaned back in his chair and sighed. As chairman of the director's board of UBS Group AG, he had worked hard to restore trust and confidence in the world's largest wealth management bank. UBS Group AG had worked through some difficult issues in the last few years, but this time everything seemed different. In terms of the general economic situation and the banking industry in particular, Europe was still losing ground to the United States. Axel Weber got out of his chair, grabbed the report again and took a closer look at Europe's ten largest banks. While walking around his office, one point in particular attracted his attention. He considered briefly, then strode across the room to the telephone. He called a longtime friend and asked him to hurry over. Axel Weber wanted to talk to him for a special reason. The point that had attracted his attention was that many of the banks ranked higher than the UBS Group AG were obviously all pursuing a specific strategy. There was a knock on the door and Martin Blessing entered the office. Axel Weber offered his friend a chair and explained his idea for the UBS Group AG. Acquiring another bank could help to cope with future challenges in the banking market and simultaneously push the UBS Group AG to the top of the rankings. Martin Blessing immediately proposed a suitable acquisition partner: Commerzbank AG. As the former CEO of this financial institute, Blessing initiated and surveilled the restructuring of Germany's second largest retail bank in person and had good insight into its processes. But the friends wanted to be absolutely sure about the success of their plan and therefore hired a well experienced team of investment banking analysts to assess the acquisition more closely. First of all, current circumstances had to be examined to provide the team with all the necessary information for their task. The UBS inhouse consulting department went to work.

2 Background Knowledge

2.1 Economy

The global economy was hit hard after the crisis in 2007 and recovery is still in progress. Compared to Europe, however, the US recovery seems much faster. This is owing to a variety of factors.

Macroeconomic development has been one crucial driver of the widening gap between the two sides of the Atlantic. Post crisis, US GDP growth rate has been constantly positive and a big factor in the divergence in economic development between the US and Europe. Since 2010, growth rates of 2–2.5% p.a. were the rule rather than the exception, leaving Europe far behind (Fig. 3). This growth was driven almost entirely by private consumption, a traditional pillar of the US economy. The property sector, however, is no longer the main engine of the US economy and remains, despite overall positive development in 2015, volatile.

Another factor in the positive development of the US economy is the unemployment rate, as a lagging indicator of economic development. Unemployment rates in the US have fallen significantly to 4.9% in early 2016, while wages have been rising over the past few years.[1] In terms of currency, the US dollar has been robust which has also strengthened the economy. By contrast, the very existence of the euro has been called into question several times, spreading the fear of a breakup of the monetary union.[2] Europe's economy has been stumbling since the crisis and has had to cope with some internal difficulties. For instance, the dramatic economic weakness of regions like Greece, Spain, Portugal and Cyprus has negatively affected the European corporate confidence, which is one of the major reasons for Europe's sluggish economic recovery.

In terms of the political environment, the European Union continues to struggle with major conflicts of interest between the independent member states. Agreements must be unanimously ratified by all 28 members, thus slowing down many decision making processes. This handicaps economic growth. The US, with a more

[1] See Auswärtiges Amt (2016).

[2] See Schildbach (2013).

centralized government of common interest, is able to react more quickly to global economic changes.

In summary, the increasing divergence between the US and the European economy is multi-factorial, including political effects as well as macroeconomic developments. This is also reflected in their respective financial institutions.

2.2 Banking Industry

As far as the banking industry is concerned, banks play a central role in economies. As they manage money from savers and provide credit to other actors, such as businesses and individuals. They influence the economy and are at the same time affected by it.

During the financial crisis, a lot of weaker US banks collapsed and disappeared. This had a more or less self-healing effect on the banking business in the US. It resulted in fewer but even stronger players. On the other hand, many European banks had to be rescued by national financial agencies, keeping unprofitable banks alive. Furthermore, while newly enforced regulatory requirements protect them from future insolvency, they also allow them almost no space to be profitable. Therefore, today's banking situation in the EU is marked by many small and unprofitable banks which are, due to further regulation, weak and struggling. As a result, European banks are pursuing a strategy of consolidation. Bigger banks acquire smaller, weaker competitors and integrate them into their own businesses. This process raises the profitability level, creates cost and revenue synergies, and also contributes to bigger client bases for the main players in the European banking sector.[3]

Numerous examples bear this out, from HSBC's acquisition of one of the top four banks in the UK, to the most recent takeover of Postbank by Deutsche Bank on the German market, which pushed Deutsche Bank a notch further up the rankings.

According to Sergio Ermotti, the Chief Executive Officer of UBS Group, the financial systems of Europe and the US are "apples and pears".[4] The main difference is the larger securitization market in the US, enabling banks to pass on credit risks by bundling loans into tradable securities. In the years 2004–2007, i.e. before the financial crisis, the net profits of the top banks on both sides of the Atlantic were at roughly the same level. This has changed completely as European banks, in contrast to US banks, seem to have never recovered from the slump in 2008. In 2015, US banks reported record profits. Their consolidated net income increased by 136% from about 82 billion euros in 2014 to a post crisis maximum of 194 billion euros. The top European banks increased their consolidated profit in 2015 by 50% from 24 billion euros in 2014 to 36 billion euros in 2015, once again clearly trailing the top US banks (Fig. 4).[5]

---

[3]See Weber (2016).

[4]See Bloomberg (2015).

[5]See Ernst&Young (2015).

The financial crisis demonstrated that even small and seemingly unimportant banks may bring large parts of the financial system into difficulties. How? Systemic crises are the result of contagion effects, which may follow as a direct consequence of contractual obligations between banks. The default of a relatively small bank may thus cause healthy banks to struggle as well. Weak players can be a threat to the stability of the whole system. The financial crisis revealed weaknesses in financial regulation. Lack of transparency and inadequate regulation led to the expansion of the crisis to countries all across Europe, which then had to rescue financial institutions using public funds. For this reason, the regulatory environment in the EU has seen a dramatic shift from lax to quite tough, and is consequently less profitable. The aim of the restrictions and regulatory requirements is to prevent this kind of disaster occurring again and to ensure stability in the markets. One of the main tools in accomplishing this task is Basel III (or the third Basel Accord), which contains a framework of requirements, e.g. capital adequacy, stress testing and market liquidity risk, for the global regulation of banks agreed by the Basel Committee of the Bank for International Settlements. Basel III is based on the antecedent Basel II regulations but with more stringent guidelines (Fig. 5). It is intended to strengthen bank capital requirements by increasing bank liquidity and decreasing bank leverage.

New technologies and new providers ("FinTech companies") are reshaping the rules in the banking sector. There are emerging technologies, such as new information platforms, which are improving connectivity among market constituents, making the markets more liquid, accessible, and efficient. The established players in the banking business either have to build up their own technologies or have to cooperate with the new entrants to the market. Collaboration between regulators, new entrants and the established players will be crucial to understanding how the new technologies work and benefitting from them.[6] Nowadays, nearly two-thirds (63%) of all bank customers worldwide use fintech products or services. At the same time, customers are more willing to recommend fintech providers to their friends and family (55%) than their bank (38%).[7]

3 Future Partners at a Glance

The current economic situation in Europe in general and especially in the European banking industry calls for further consolidation. For strong players, acquisition is one way to increase their profits and to satisfy the demand of their shareholders for acceptable returns. However, quantitative measures are not the only consideration in an acquisition. Assessing and comparing the global footprint and cultural background of future partners as well as the strategic focus of the institutions is of paramount importance.

[6] See weforum.org (2015).

[7] See worldretailbankingreport.com (2016).

3.1 UBS Group AG

Since the Bank in Winterthur was founded in 1862, more than 300 financial firms have joined to form what is known as UBS.[8] Today the Swiss bank is represented by 60,099 employees in 54 countries and is the fastest growing wealth manager in the world.

Segmented into Wealth Management and Wealth Management Americas, UBS's wealth management provides ultra-high net worth and high net worth customers with individual products in order to fulfill their financial needs. At the same time, UBS operates as Universal Bank in Switzerland serving the whole spectrum of UBS's businesses: asset management, wealth management, corporate and institutional banking, personal banking and investment bank services. With a multichannel approach, UBS is a leader in these client segments. A network of offices in 22 countries shows the large scale of UBS's Asset Management segment, which offers a diversified portfolio of investments across all major traditional and alternative asset classes. Supported by research across all these classes, corporate and institutional customers are provided with innovative solutions, consultancy, execution and comprehensive access to the world's capital markets. The Corporate Center handles all control functions of the UBS Group, including legal, finance and risk control, and provides logistic and support services for all other segments. These include information and physical security, human resources, communication and information technology (Fig. 6).[9]

The recent economic development of UBS is still affected by the subprime crisis and the net loss of over CHF22 billion in 2008. Following the bail out by the Swiss National Bank, the major restructuring has been necessary to meet the Swiss "too big to fail" regulations (Fig. 7). These regulations are designed to keep the cost to taxpayers as low as possible by minimizing the need for governments to bail out systemically important financial institutes.[10] As a consequence of these restructuring efforts, UBS recovered and were able to increase their total payout per share over the last few years, generating a net profit of CHF6204 million in 2015 (Fig. 8). A segmentation of net profits in 2015 is shown in Fig. 9. Almost 45% of all profits are made in the wealth management segments, Wealth Management and Wealth Management Americas, while Personal and Corporate Banking as well as the Investment Bank segment take a share of roughly 25% each. The smallest portion in terms of net profit is contributed by Asset Management with almost 5%.

UBS is responding to the regulatory environment and evolving market with adjustments to their strategy and business portfolios. UBS's strategy builds on the strengths of all their businesses and focuses on areas in which they excel. This includes capitalizing from growth prospects in all business areas and geographic markets they operate in. The focus of all efforts is on creating a business model that

---

[8]See UBS (2012).

[9]See UBS (2015).

[10]See Finma (2014).

is better adapted to the new regulatory and market environment. The strategy centers on the preeminent wealth management business and the Universal Bank in Switzerland, and builds on the strengths of all the businesses and on the industry-leading capital position.[11]

The wealth management industry offers attractive developments with robust growth of private wealth accumulation around the world. According to the "Global Wealth Report 2015", there is an increase in the number of ultra-high net worth and high net worth people and therefore possible customers.[12] Forecasting private financial wealth until 2019, the report forecasts an increase from $155.7 trillion to $210.1 trillion (Fig. 10). The compound annual growth rates (CAGR) show high potential especially in the Asia-Pacific region, Latin America, Eastern Europe, Middle East and Africa. Western Europe, North America as well as Japan are predicted to develop with far lower growth rates for private financial wealth (Fig. 11). This and the converging client needs in Europe led to the strategic decision to consolidate European onshore and cross-border businesses. The combination of the strategic focus on wealth management, unique footprint and capabilities, and the leading position across the attractive ultra-high net worth and high net worth client segments enables UBS to benefit from significant scale, which will help them capture market growth and increase share of wallet. Furthermore the Investment Bank segment is cut down to low risk assets to meet the challenges of the unstable and highly volatile market environment and increasing regulatory requirements. Also, with regard to the regulatory requirements and the subdued revenue environment, there is an increase in operational cost pressure. This has forced UBS to reassess front-to-back processes, to focus on identifying potential standardization, and to rethink the ownership of value chain components.

Over the last few years, investments in financial technology have multiplied. UBS is already the largest employer in the information technology sector in Switzerland and the market expects continued digital disruption in the financial industry. UBS is focused on leveraging the technology not only to improve the services for clients, but also to increase scalability by providing more efficient methods for delivering content to directly access clients and derive the most important information from vast amounts of data for better business management.

3.2 Commerzbank AG

The history of Commerzbank goes back to the foundation of the "Commerz und Disconto-Bank in Hamburg" in 1870. With its internationalization in 1967 and presence in over 50 countries today, Commerzbank has developed into a financial services provider operating worldwide. After the acquisition of Dresdner Bank in 2009, Commerzbank operates the biggest network of branches in Germany.[13]

---

[11]See UBS (2011).

[12]See BCG (2015).

[13]See Commerzbank (2015).

The different segments in which Commerzbank serves its clients are widely spread (Fig. 12). The Private Customers segment with about 1100 branches, direct banking and 12 million customers, represents the second largest retail bank in Germany. The Mittelstandsbank is divided into three group divisions. Mittelstand Germany bundles businesses with small and medium sized customers, the public sector and regional and small and medium sized institutional customers in Germany. Corporate customers with turnovers over 500 million euros are served by the Large Corporates and International Group and the Financial Institutions Group is responsible for relationships with credit institutions in Germany and abroad, as well as with central banks.[14] Mittelstandsbank offers its customers the complete range of products of an international full-service bank: traditional credit products and customized structured financing solutions, investment and hedging products and products in the areas of cash management and international business. The Central and Eastern Europe segment of Commerzbank includes all activities in universal and direct banking in Central and Eastern Europe represented by the mBank brand. This comprises serving customers in retail, corporate and investment banking in Poland, the Czech Republic and Slovakia.

The investment banking activities of Commerzbank are bundled in the Corporates and Markets segment, which serves not only Corporates and Markets customers, but also customers of other Group segments. The last segment of Commerzbank is the non-core asset run-off segment, where the Commercial Real Estate Portfolio (CRE; 10.3 billion euros), the ship financing portfolio (Deutsche Schiffsbank, DSB; 8.4 billion euros) and the Public Finance portfolio (44.2 billion euros) are bundled in the Group divisions. The Commerzbank bad asset run-off strategy aims to systematically reduce the individual segment portfolios in a way that preserves value and minimizes risk. The aim of this asset reduction is to free up capital so that it can be employed in business areas offering higher returns.[15]

In the financial crisis, Commerzbank was rescued by the German Federal Agency for Financial Market Stabilisaton (FSMA) in 2008. Over 10 billion euros were paid out to prevent the collapse of Commerzbank. The German Federal Republic with 15% is therefore the biggest non-institutional shareholder followed by BlackRock and Deutsche Bank with 5% each (Fig. 13). Since then, the operating profits have stabilized thanks to cost saving and lean process programs, and increased to 1.9 billion euros in 2015, which represents its highest post crisis value. Despite the recovery of Commerzbank in terms of operating profits, its performance at the German stock exchange has not followed the positive development of the DAX index (Fig. 14).

The strategic outlook for Commerzbank is clear. In a persistingly tough market environment, the private customer segment was able to acquire around 287,000 new customers, leading to a major increase in private banking operating profits of 65% from 455 million euros in 2014 to 752 million euros in 2015 (Fig. 15). The strategic

[14]See Commerzbank (2016).

[15]See Commerzbank (2016).

realignment of the Private Customer business is a key element in the plan to boost earnings. The goal is to unite modern technologies with traditional values, such as fairness, trust and competence. This includes investments in Commerzbank's platform, its product and service offering, the advisory process and training employees in the Private Customer business to raise revenues per customer as well as the number of customers.[16] Besides the Private Customers Segment, the strategy focuses on the Mittelstandsbank, which is the most profitable segment of the total operating profits at 38% (Fig. 16). The Mittelstandsbank will continue expanding its successful business model and leading market position. Growth will focus on the acquisition of new customers, particularly in the small and medium-sized corporate customers segment and on the expansion of business with existing customers in Germany.[17]

The run-off strategy for the new Asset and Capital Recovery Unit (ACR) segment will be rigorously pursued in the upcoming years. The aim is to still run off the remaining portfolios and residual risks completely over time in a way that preserves value and releases capital. Opportunities to sell assets and portfolios will therefore continue to be taken in cases where a sale makes economic sense. By the end of 2019, the ACR segment aims to further reduce the CRE and DSB portfolios substantially to below 5 billion euros. This represents a reduction of around 50% compared with the value of the portfolios at the time of the transfer, which was just under 10 billion euros.

Commerzbank intends to transfer a large part of the remaining assets—exclusively unimpaired assets with high internal ratings—to the Private Customers and Mittelstandsbank segments and to the Others and Consolidation division. The criteria for the transfer of assets are good credit quality, low volatility of income and the ability to integrate the assets into the refinancing and liquidity structure of the units concerned.[18]

4 Quantitative Analysis

Besides growth prospects, strategic fitness and possible downsides, the evaluation of the company to be acquired and the value creation of an acquisition are major issues that have to be assessed and taken into account long before the actual deal. This quantitative analysis of an acquisition is complicated, especially in the banking industry.

[16] See Commerzbank (2013).

[17] See Commerzbank (2013).

[18] See Commerzbank (2016).

4.1 Valuation of Commerzbank AG

The quantitative analysis starts with the evaluation of the bank to be acquired—in this case Commerzbank. Since it is hard to define annual cash flows, the number of applicable evaluation methods besides market capitalization is limited. In order to assess a fair value and a possible undervaluation of Commerzbank, the Dividend Discount Model (DDM), verified by a multiple method, might prove to be the most appropriate (Figs. 17 and 18). A fair valuation is important in structuring the deal structure and, of course, the purchase price. The purchase price consists of the market capitalization and a premium, as incentive for current shareholders to sell their shares. With regard to the deal and given a possible undervaluation of Commerzbank, UBS might be able and willing to pay a higher premium.

4.2 Value Creation

On one side of the quantitative analysis of the value creation are all the expenses to be considered. These include the purchase price, as well as restructuring costs incurred. On the other side, there are all the revenues produced by the acquisition. The combination of these constitutes the deal value, taking into account a possible undervaluation of Commerzbank, and the assumed cost and revenue synergies realized over a period of 10 years.[19] According to UBS's Corporate Center controlling division, the restructuring costs of merging the two financial institutes can be estimated at 1.4 billion euros. Opposed to this, the cost and revenue synergies have been estimated for the pro forma financial statement, giving a conservative run rate of under 1 billion euros (Fig. 19). Further the realization of cost synergies is expected to reach 78% in the third year after the acquisition (Figs. 20 and 21).[20]

4.3 Strategic Decision

After evaluating both qualitative and quantitative aspects of the acquisition of Commerzbank by UBS, a decision has to be made about the circumstances of the acquisition. Having reviewed all of the data and material gathered, the consulting team determined that if an acquisition were to proceed, the value creation must exceed 25% of the evaluated fair value of Commerzbank.[21] This threshold calculation would produce clear values concerning market capitalization premium and therefore purchase price under which an acquisition of Commerzbank would be reasonable.

[19] See Strutz (2008).

[20] See Strutz (2008).

[21] See Biagosch (2016).

5 Executive Summary

After four weeks, the inhouse consulting team handed in their report, comprising two major parts. They examined issues the banking markets in Europe and beyond the Atlantic Ocean were facing and had a close look at (the) future partners in terms of their business models, structural organizations and strategies for the future. Axel Weber and Martin Blessing read the report carefully and with great interest. This information should be sufficient for the investment banking team to work with. The very next day a team of analysts was assembled in Axel Weber's office. He briefly introduced them to the task, handing over the report with a list of four questions to be answered. The analysts, eager to take on the exciting challenge, went to work immediately. The team split into three task-oriented sub-teams to, respectively, assess the economic situation, evaluate the future partners in terms of fit, and determine the financial scope of the acquisition.

6 Your Task

Axel Weber is expecting a clear recommendation of the investment banking team, you are now part of. Find the answer to the question whether the UBS Group AG should acquire the Commerzbank AG, by doing the following:

I. Name problems the banking market in Europe is facing and evaluate consequences of an acquisition of Commerzbank AG for the UBS Group.
II. Compare the strategic focus of Commerzbank AG and UBS Group and identify the implications for the acquisition.
III. Determine whether Commerzbank AG is currently over-/undervalued and verify your result with one appropriate method.
IV. Calculate the value the acquisition creates for the UBS Group and derive a possible purchase price for Commerzbank AG.

7 Appendix

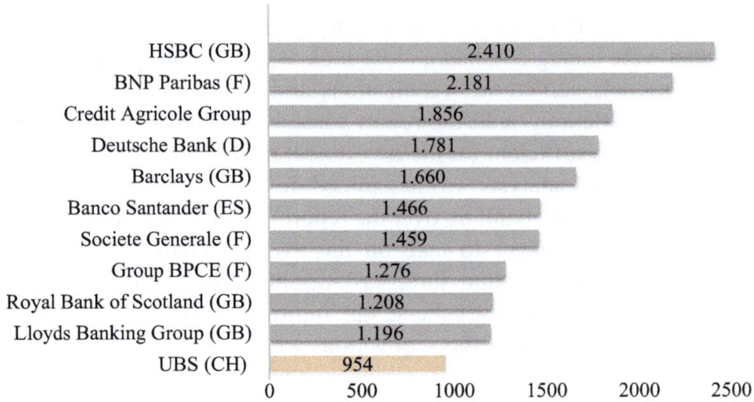

Fig. 1 UBS's position in Europe by total assets, 2016 (€bn) (see Statista 3 2016)

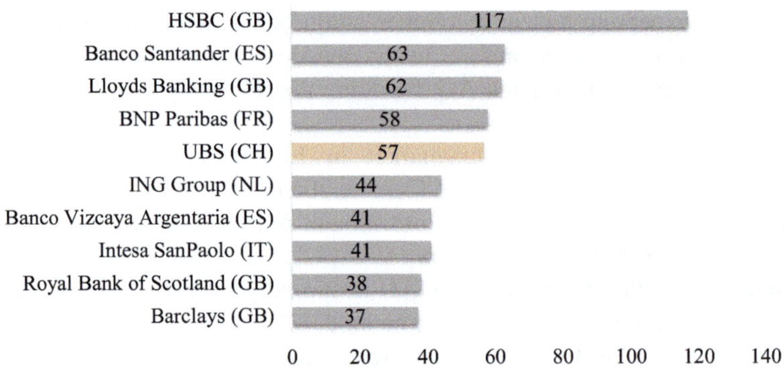

Fig. 2 UBS's position in Europe by market capitalisation, 2016 (€bn) (see Statista 1 2016)

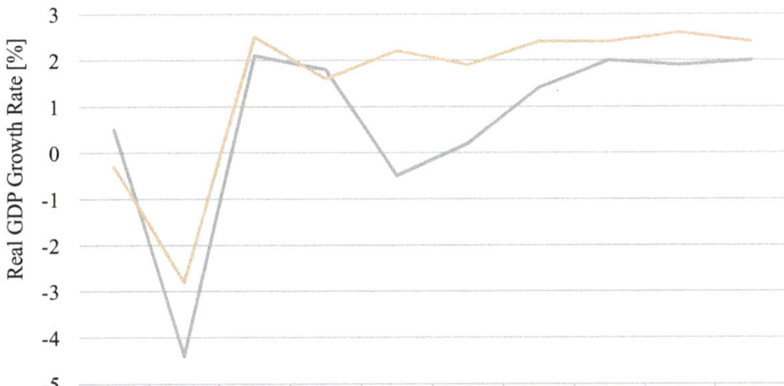

	2008	2009	2010	2011	2012	2013	2014	2015	2016E	2017E
EU	0.5	-4.4	2.1	1.8	-0.5	0.2	1.4	2	1.9	2
US	-0.3	-2.8	2.5	1.6	2.2	1.9	2.4	2.4	2.6	2.4

Fig. 3 Annual growth rate of the real GDP of Europe in comparison to the US (%) [Own analysis based on information from Eurostat (2015), Statista 2 (2016), European Commission (2016)]

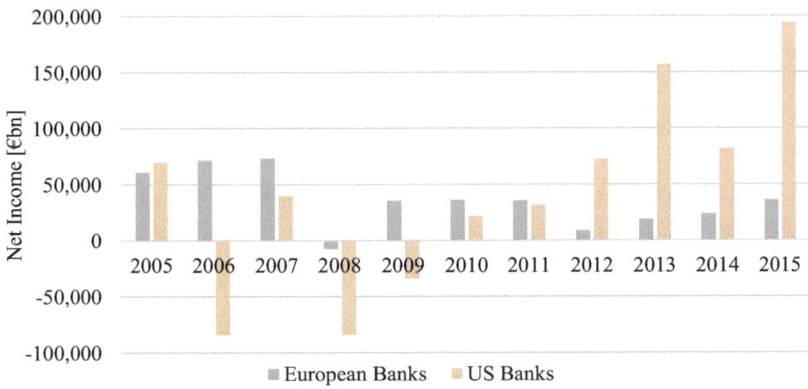

Fig. 4 Net income of the ten largest banks in Europe and in the US (€bn) [Own analysis based on annual reports, Ernst&Young (2015)]

Basel II	Requirements	Basel III*
8%	Minimum Ratio of Total Capital to RWAs	**10.5%**
2%	Minimum Ratio of Common equity to RWAs	**4.5% to 7%**
4%	Tier 1 Capital to RWAs	**6%**
2%	Core Tier 1 Capital to RWAs	**5%**
None	Capital Conservation Buffer to RWAs	**2.5%**
None	Leverage Ratio	**3%**
None	Countercyclical Buffer	**0% to 2.5%**
None	Minimum Liquidity Coverage Ratio	**TBD (2015)**
None	Minimum Net Stable Funding Ratio	**TBD (2018)**
None	Systematically Important Financial Institutions Charge	**TBD (2011)**

***Basel III requirements will be progressively phased-in over the next eight years**

Fig. 5 Requirements of Basel III in comparison to Basel II (see riskarticles.com 2011)

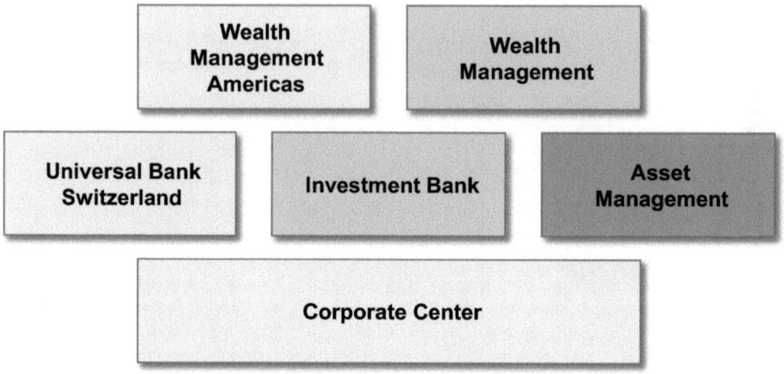

Fig. 6 UBS Group AG structure by its segments (see UBS 2015)

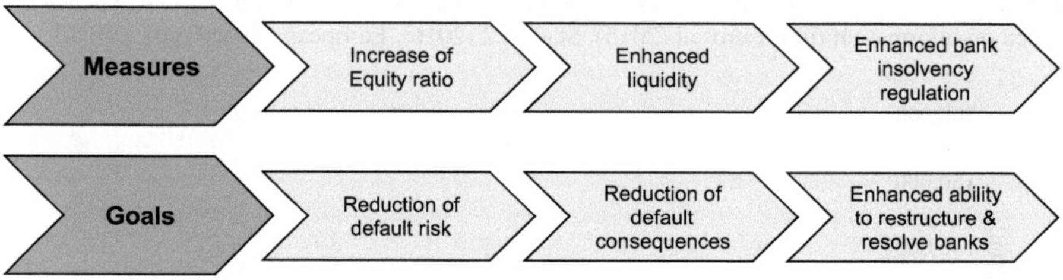

Fig. 7 Too-Big-to-Fail-Regime in Switzerland (see Finma 2014)

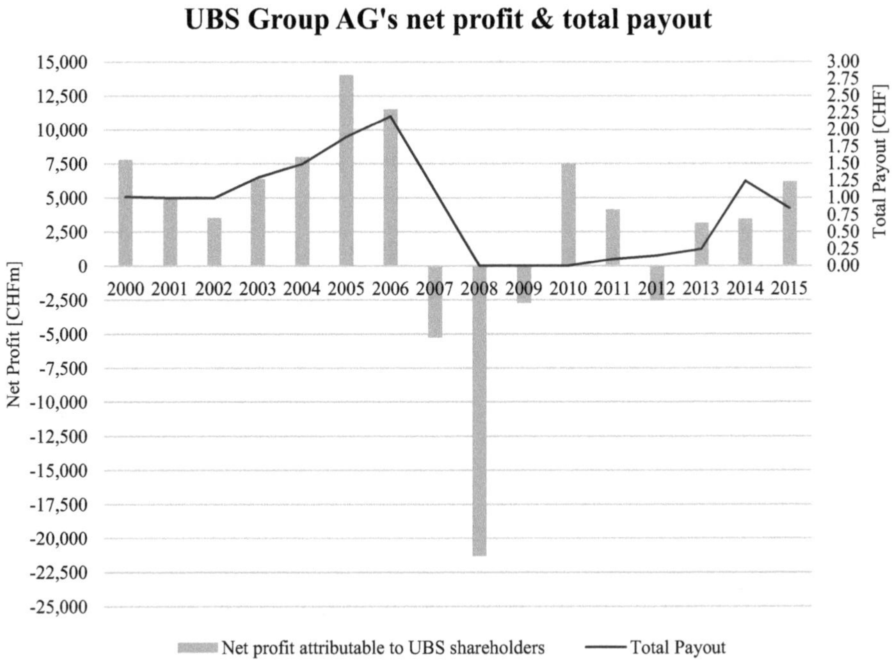

Fig. 8 UBS Group AG's performance—net profit (CHFm) and total payout (CHF) (UBS Group AG, annual reports 2000–2015)

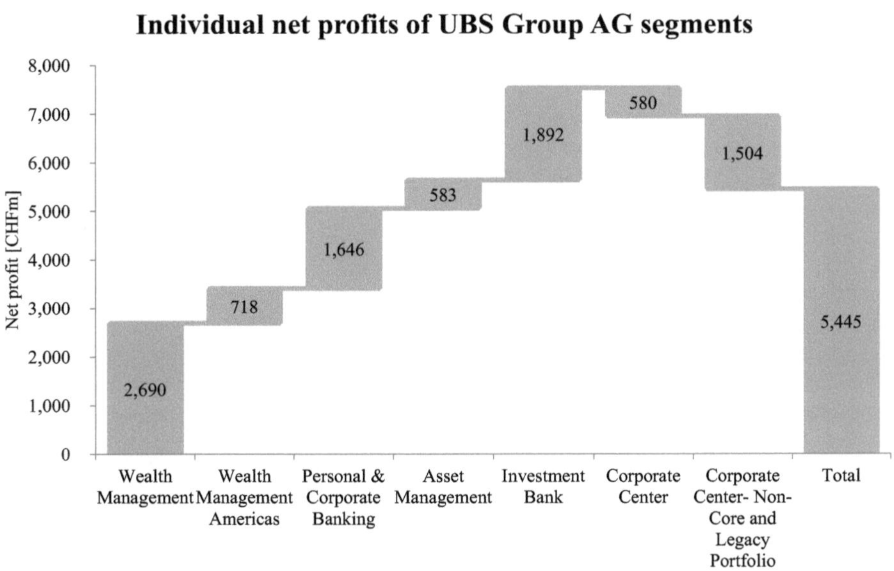

Fig. 9 UBS Group AG segments and their corresponding net profits (CHFm), 2015 (see UBS 2016)

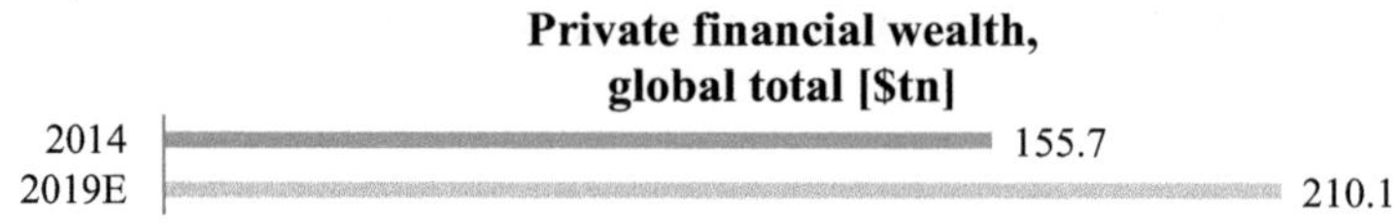

Fig. 10 Estimated development of the global private financial wealth (see BCG 2015)

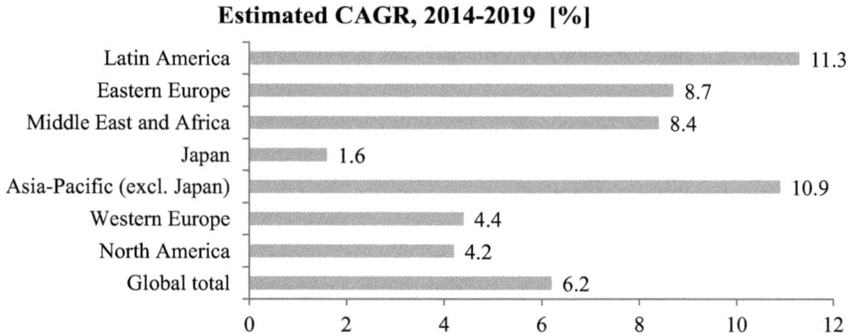

Fig. 11 Expected growth of the global wealth management business in the next years (see BCG 2015)

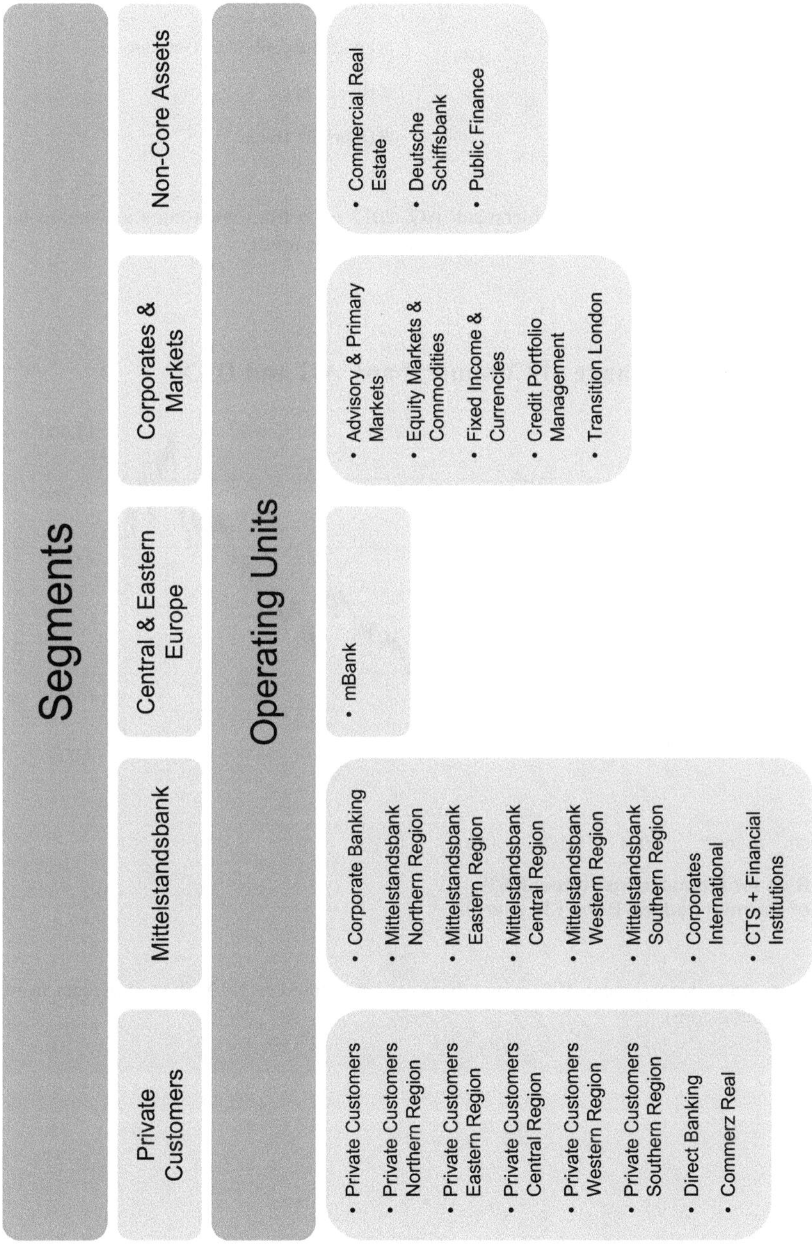

Fig. 12 Organisational structure of the Commerzbank AG (see Commerzbank 2016)

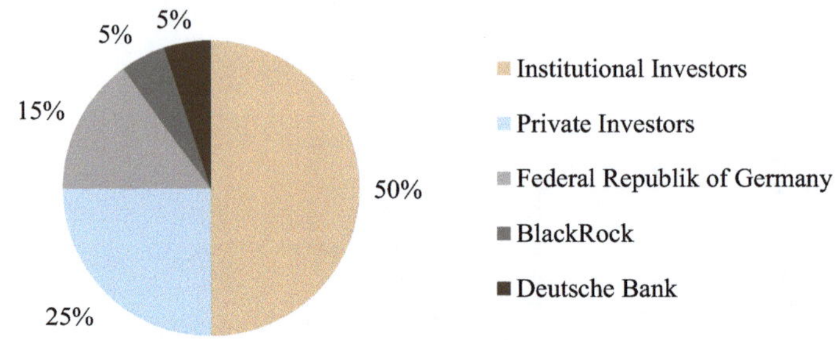

Fig. 13 Shareholder structure of Commerzbank AG, 2015 (data from www.commerzbank.com/en/hauptnavigation/aktionaere/aktie/aktionaersstruktur/aktionaere.html)

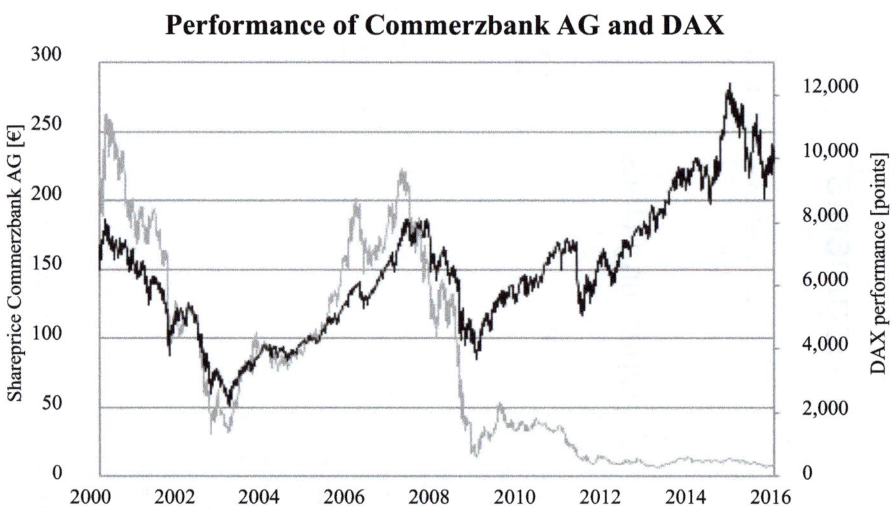

Market Risk for Financial Institutes: 6.0%
Return of German Federal Bond (30 years): 0.961%

Fig. 14 Share price development of Commerzbank AG compared to DAX (historical data from www.finance.yahoo.com)

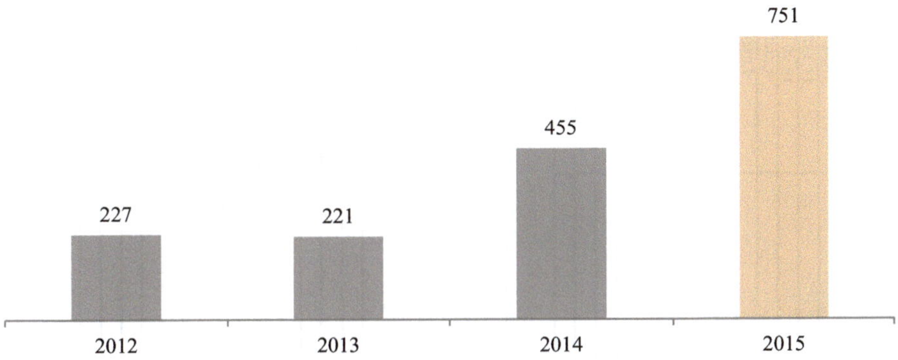

Fig. 15 Commerzbank AG's operating profit in private banking (see Commerzbank 2016)

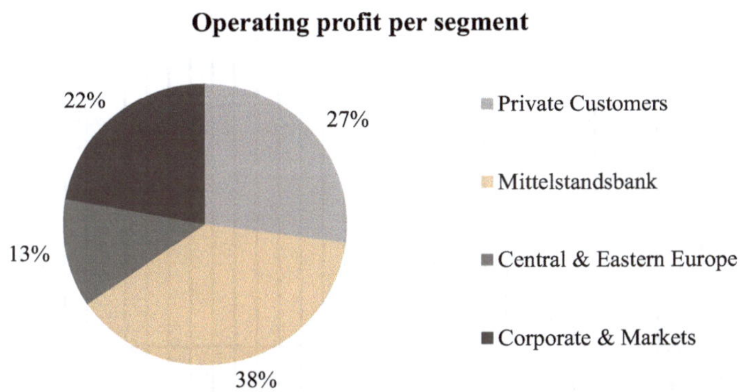

Fig. 16 Differentiation of Commerzbank AG's operating profit, 2015 (see Commerzbank 2016)

	Year 2015	Year 2016	Year 2017	Year 2018
Total Revenues [€m]	9,780	9,469	9,806	10,090
Operating Profit [€m]	1,909	1,668	1,966	2,194
Net Profit [€m]	1,062	1,093	1,311	1,474
Dividend [€]	0.20	0.26	0.36	0.47
RWA [€bn]	198.20	196.90	199.80	201.60

Fig. 17 Estimations of the development of the Commerzbank AG's net profit and other figures [Analysts' Estimates (2016) Commerzbank AG]

Bank	Share price [€]	EPS [€]	Beta	Equity [€m]	Book Value/ Share [€]	Shares Outstanding [m]
Commerzbank AG	6.67	0.81	1.30	21,090	23.50	1,252
Deutsche Bank	14.46	-5.19	1.31	74,970	54.53	1,370
Santander	3.97	0.45	1.29	98,780	6.83	14,390
Uni Credit	2.39	0.27	1.68	54,750	8.53	6,083
Bankia	0.76	0.09	2.13	14,160	1.10	11,517
BNP Paribas	43.10	5.14	1.47	96,751	79.00	1,246
Credit Suisse	10.51	-2.50	1.46	46,600	24.02	1,950

Fig. 18 Key figures of large European banks (www.finanzen.net)

	UBS Group AG [CHFm]	Commerzbank AG [€m]	Proforma [€m]	Expected total synergies	UBS New [€m]
Income					
Net interest income	6,732	5,779	11,858	1.10%	**11,988**
Credit loss (expense) / recovery	-117	-696	-802	-	**-802**
Net interest income after credit loss expense	**6,615**	**5,083**	**11,056**	-	**11,187**
Net fee and commission income	17,140	3,424	18,901	-	**18,901**
Net trading income	5,742	499	5,684	-	**5,684**
Other income	1,107	60	1,060	-	**1,060**
Total operating income	**30,604**	**9,066**	**36,701**	-	**36,832**
Personnel expenses					
Salaries	5,970	3,670	9,061	1.41%	**8,933**
Total variable compensation	3,410	0	3,079	-	**3,079**
WMA: Financial advisor compensation	3,552	0	3,207	-	**3,207**
other personnel expenses (Social security, pensions)	2,613	230	2,590	-	**2,590**
Total	**15,545**	**3,900**	**17,937**	-	**17,809**
General administrative					
Occupancy	930	604	1,444	1.59%	**1,421**
Rent/maintanance of IT/other equipment	510	482	943	30.66%	**654**
Communication & market data service	611	254	806	6.08%	**757**
Administration	718	153	801	3.87%	**770**
Marketing & public relations	486	167	439	5.47%	**415**
Travel & entertainment	460	329	744	5.24%	**705**
Professional fees	1,354	428	1,651	3.33%	**1,596**
Outsourcing of IT/other services	1,743	372	1,574	1.21%	**1,555**
Provisions for litigation, regulatory, similar matters	1,087	279	1,261	3.33%	**1,219**
other	208	230	418	5.03%	**397**
Total	**8,107**	**2,759**	**10,080**	-	**9,488**
Depreciation/ impairment of property, equipment & software	908	89	820	-	**820**
Amortization/ Impairment of intangible assets	94	210	384	-	**384**
Total operating expenses (reported)	**25,115**	**7,157**	**29,836**	-	**28,501**
Net Profit					
Operating profit/(loss) before tax	**5,489**	**1,909**	**6,866**	-	7,486
Tax expense/(benefit)	-898	732	-79	-	-79
Net profit/ (loss)	**6,387**	**1,177**	**6,944**	-	**7,564**
Net profit/ (loss) attributable to non-controlling interests	-183	-115	-50	-	-50
Net Profit attributable to UBS Group AG shareholders	**6,204**	**1,062**	**6,664**	-	**7,514**

Fig. 19 Proforma financial statement (see Commerzbank 2016; UBS 2016)

	Year 1	Year 2	Year 3	Year 4	Year 5
Cost Synergies	€85 m (12%)	€290 m (40%)	€560 m (78%)	€720 m (100%)	€720 m (100%)
Restructuring Costs	€700 m (50%)	€370 m (26%)	€210 m (15%)	€100 m (7%)	€20 m (1%)

Fig. 20 Realization of synergies in case of acquisition

Segments	CEO	Private Customers	Mittelstands bank	CEE	Corporates & Markets	Non-Core Assets	Others	Total Group
Members of board/ CEO	50	-	-	-	-	-	-	50
Number of employees	-	15,381	5,482	7,960	1,944	491	17,324	48,582
Total wages [€m]	16.61	1,132.45	507.98	194.32	442.58	64.71	1,472.51	3,831.16
o/w: variable wages [€m]	6.87	44.55	36.79	40.57	112.02	8.02	89.51	338.33

Fig. 21 Salaries of the Commerzbank AG in 2014 (Commerzbank AG's compensation report 2014)

8 Solution

8.1 Need for Action

Macroeconomic development

In contrast to the EU, the US economy is experiencing a slight boom in the aftermath of the financial crisis. This can be seen from the constantly high GDP growth rates, the falling unemployment rates, a stable currency and a favorable political environment.

Differences in markets

While in the US, the financial crisis led to the disappearance of weaker market players and therefore to a dramatic consolidation of the market, the European rescue programs and newly introduced regulations prevented that from happening. US banks emerged from the crisis stronger and are able to exploit the positive economic development with a greater variety of complex financial products. In the eyes of many experts, Europe is "overbanked", leaving little room to be profitable.

Regulation

The harsh European regulations set high requirements for equity ratios, liquidity, resolvability and transparency of business processes. To meet these requirements and to build up extra monetary pillars, additional administrative efforts and higher revenues are needed. This, in combination with the slow macroeconomic development of Europe, allows no room for errors or even growth.

Strategy—Acquisition as opportunity

Acquisitions represent an important opportunity for growth, especially in the "overbanked" European market. This enables strong players to diversify both their strategy and their overall footprint and gives them the chance to overcome challenges like regulation and poor market environment by building on the strengths of a bigger entity.

8.2 Limited Strategic Fit

UBS is focused on the Universal Bank, with its presence in Switzerland only, and the global wealth management business with ultra-high net worth and high net worth clients to exploit the significant growth in global private wealth. On the other hand, Commerzbank centers its strategic efforts on the private-customer business in Germany and Eastern Europe, its expertise in the Mittelstandsbank segment and the unpopular non-core asset run off segment.

In light of this, the two banks have complementary footprints and strategic outlooks and therefore lack an overlap in terms of markets, clients and business model. For an acquisition this limited strategic fit complicates the assessment of potential cost and revenue synergies.

8.3 Valuation of Commerzbank AG

Dividend discount model

The valid calculation of a fair market value for the Commerzbank AG requires some advance thinking. Due to the fact that it is hard to define key figures for capital expenditures, debt and working capital for financial institutes, a regular discounted cash flow model does not seem to be the appropriate way to value a bank. For this reason, a dividend discount model (DDM) was used, assuming the fair value of a stock to be the present value of the corresponding dividends. In a basic DDM, the expected dividends are discounted by the costs of equity of the firm, resulting in a stock price that, multiplied by the number of outstanding shares, yields the company's fair market value. So first of all a very conservative growth rate of 1% from the year 2019 on has been added to the dividends of Commerzbank AG, estimated from 2015 to 2018. Commerzbank AG was expected to make further recoveries from the financial crisis in 2008, yielding the unlikeliness of a "no-growth scenario". The growth rate made the DDM more realistic and the low rate of 1% should prevent the risk of overvaluing the bank. The costs of equity of Commerzbank AG were calculated according to the equation shown in Fig. 22. The return of a German Federal Bond (30 years) served as the risk free rate of 0.916%. The average return over the first half of the year 2016 was used to reduce the impact of single economic or political events as much as possible. The beta-factor of

Cost of Equity

$$r_e = r_f + \beta_i * (E(r_m) - r_f)$$

r_f: Risk Free Rate
β_i: Beta-factor
$E(r_m)$: Market Risk

Dividend Discount Model

$$\sum_{t=1}^{t=n} \frac{DPS_t}{(1+r_e)^t} + \frac{DPS_{n+1}}{(r_e - g)(1+r_e)^n}$$

DPS: Dividend per share
r_e: Costs of Equity
g: Growth rate

Fig. 22 Formulas needed to calculate the DDM

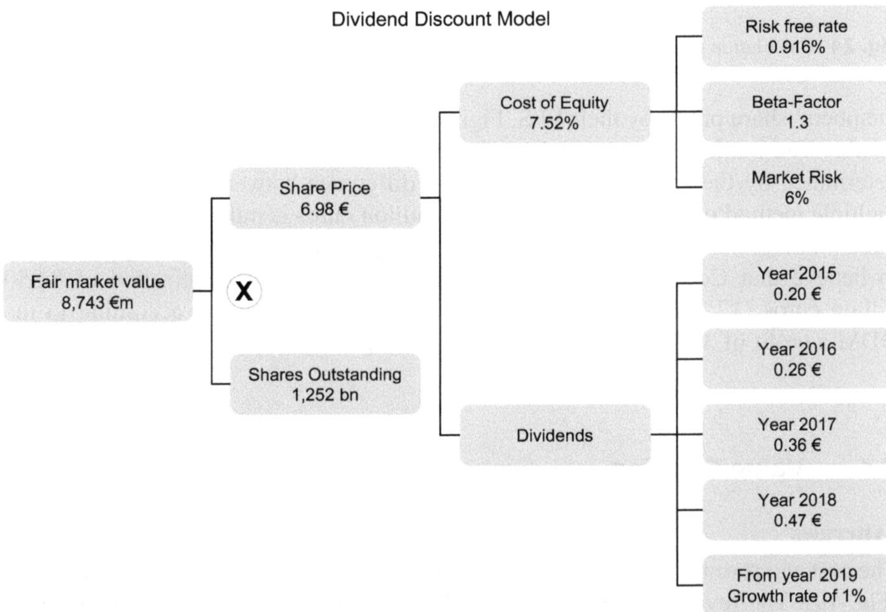

Fig. 23 Derivation of the FMV of the Commerzbank AG by the DDM

Commerzbank AG, fitting to many sources, was set to 1.3 and the market risk, according to the FAUB between 5.5% and 7% for financial institutes, to 6%. The DDM yielded a stock price of 6.98 € for Commerzbank AG, which is shown in Fig. 23. Multiplying the fair stock price of 6.98 € by the 1.252 billion shares outstanding, the Commerzbank AG's fair market value is 8.743 billion euros.

Multiple method

Multiples are a rather simple but valid form to check the fair market value of Commerzbank AG for significance. Thereby a peer group of financial institutes has been created, matching the business model and financial situation of the second largest retail bank in Germany best. The peer group consisting of four institutes is shown in Fig. 24. Then the group's P/E ratio has been calculated, dividing the

Bank	Share price [€]	EPS [€]	P/E Ratio
Commerzbank AG	6.67	0.81	8.23
Santander	3.97	0.45	8.82
Uni Credit	2.39	0.27	8.85
Bankia	0.76	0.09	8,.44
BNP Paribas	43.1	5.14	8.39
		Mean	8.62
		Median	8.63

MCAP (mean) = 8,748 €m
[=8.62 * 0.81 € * 1,252 mio. shares outstanding]

MCAP (median) = 8,755 €m
[=8.63 € * 0.81 * 1,252 mio. shares outstanding]

Commerzbank AG undervalued

8.743 €m (FMV)
- 8.351€m (MCAP)
392 €m

Fig. 24 Calculation of the MCAP of the Commerzbank AG using a multiple method

members' share prices by their EPS. Figure 24 shows the respective calculation and results. The market value according to the multiple is slightly larger than the one determined by the DDM. Nevertheless, the difference between the DDM and the multiple method of 5 million euros and 12 million euros is rather small, sufficiently underpinning the significance of the DDM. Furthermore, both methods give reasons to believe that Commerzbank AG with a current market capitalization of 8.350 billion euros (1252 billion shares × 6.68 €) is undervalued. So according to the DDM a profit of 392 million euros can be made just by acquisition.

8.4 Value Creation

Synergies

The cost and revenue synergies were deducted from the proforma financial statement (Fig. 19). The revenue synergies were calculated on the assumption of gaining an extra 1.10% of net interest income, leading to a total amount of 130 million euros p.a. The cost synergies can be divided into three major parts: personnel, IT, general administrative. These add up to total savings of 720 million euros p.a. Thus we monetized total synergies of 850 million euros p.a.

However, there are also dis-synergies that must not be forgotten when considering an acquisition. First of all, uniting the personnel of both banks and setting a common goal requires considerable effort. This takes time and often leads to a reduction of performance in almost all segments, having a direct impact on the bank's profits. Besides this critical step in implementation there is a danger of cannibalizing UBS Switzerland AG's universal banking. Due to the fact that Commerzbank AG has branches in Switzerland too, they might be drawn into competition with UBS Switzerland AG, reducing one another's profits. Dis-synergies are very hard to determine and therefore they are only partially included in the mathematical model in terms of restructuring costs. It is nevertheless important to be aware of them (Fig. 25).

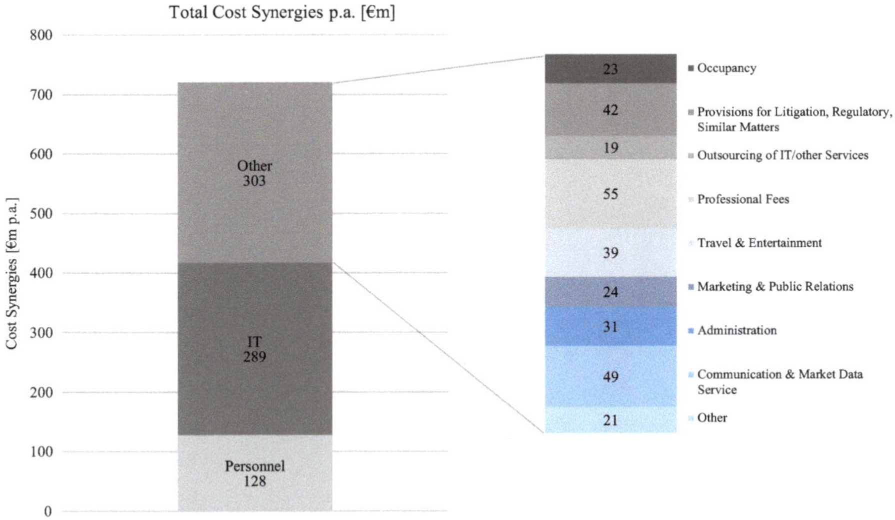

Fig. 25 Total cost synergies per year in detail

Restructuring costs

As already mentioned earlier, additional costs are incurred by implementing the new structure of the bank. Here, once again, the expected restructuring costs of past acquisitions in the European banking market have been benchmarked. Even though the restructuring costs listed in the respective balance sheets together lay beneath the originally expected amounts, higher costs have been assumed to avoid the risk of overvaluing the acquisition, when calculating the net present value (NPV). So they have been set to 1400 million euros, the second largest amount according to the benchmark.

NPV

Since the total cost synergies and restructuring costs are not expected to kick in immediately, they have been distributed according to the information gained from past acquisitions over a period of 4 and 5 years respectively. Cost synergies have been distributed in an increasing manner, the restructuring costs in a decreasing manner to reflect the real outcome as precisely as possible. The individual steps of the ramp up are shown in Fig. 26.

In contrast, the revenue synergies are expected to be achievable from the day of acquisition on due to the positive reputation of the UBS Group AG. In Fig. 26 the resulting net cash flows are shown. It is clear that by the second year after the acquisition the synergies outperform the restructuring costs, reaching the total synergy run rate of 850 million euros p.a. in the fourth year.

To calculate the NPV of the acquisition, the net cash flows have been discounted over a period of 10 years, in the expectation that the synergy run rate stays the same

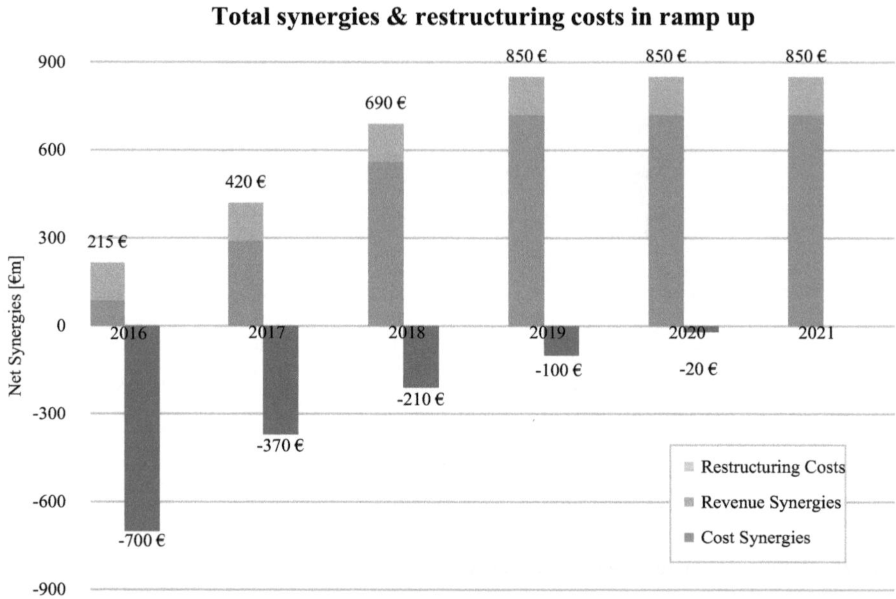

Fig. 26 Ramp-up of annual synergies and restructuring costs

NPV Calculation

$$\sum_{t=1}^{t=10} \frac{\text{Net Synergies}_t}{\text{WACC}_{\text{UBS Group AG}})^t} = 3{,}330\ €m$$

Fig. 27 Calculation of the NPV, resulting in the acquisition of the Commerzbank AG

after year 4, by UBS's weighted average cost of capital (WACC) of 9.81%. This yields an NPV of 3330 million euros and therewith a clear recommendation to acquire Commerzbank AG. The calculation is shown in Fig. 27. The IRR of 19%, calculated under the same circumstances as the NPV with MS Excel, clearly toward the WACC, underpinning the statement of the NPV.

Purchase price

At first glance, the acquisition would create a total value of 3722 million euros, the sum of the NPV and the difference between the MCAP and the FMV. But the premium to the market that would have to be paid additionally to the shareholders of Commerzbank AG had to be considered. The higher this premium, the less value would be created for the UBS Group. Figure 28 shows the relation between value creation and the premium, which depends on the MCAP. It becomes obvious that beyond a premium of 44%, no value is created at all. So to determine the maximum premium the UBS Group AG should be willing to pay, a minimum value to be reached by acquiring Commerzbank AG was set. This minimum amount should

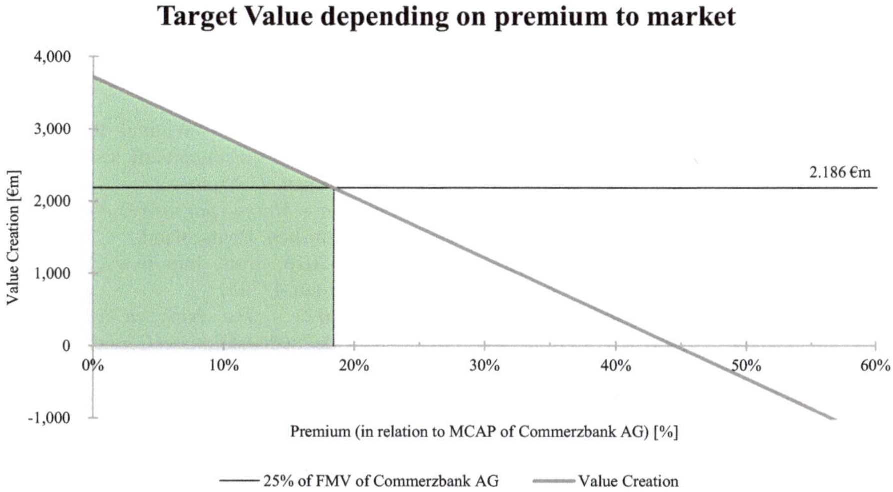

Fig. 28 Value creation of the acquisition in relation to the premium to market

Maximum Purchase Price for the Commerzbank AG

	8,351 €m (MCAP)
+	1,536 €m (Premium)
	9,887 €m

Fig. 29 Calculation of the maximum acceptable purchase price for Commerzbank AG

balance the limited strategic fit and bad assets that come with the acquisition. Twenty-five percent of the FMV of Commerzbank AG were assessed to be sufficiently large, setting the minimum value to be created at 2186 million euros. This resulted in a maximum payable premium to market of 18.4%, which were equal to 1536 million euros. The boundary and the resulting target range are shown in Fig. 28, visualized in the green colored area. Every premium within this range creates value sufficiently large to balance the risks of the acquisition. So the maximum purchase price for Commerzbank AG can be determined as 9887 million euros, as shown in Fig. 29, consisting of the current MCAP of 8350 million euros and the maximum payable premium of 1536 million euros.

The final recommendation is to acquire Commerzbank AG, if the premium to market does not exceed 1536 million euros, or, in other words, if the total purchase price for Commerzbank AG is smaller than 9887 million euros.

9 Possible Questions

- Does the obtained premium offer a realistic deal to the Commerzbank shareholders?
- Are there any other possible scenarios for an acquisition of Commerzbank?

References

Auswärtiges Amt. (2016). Accessed June 15, 2016, from http://www.auswaertiges-amt.de/DE/Aussenpolitik/Laender/Laenderinfos/USA/Wirtschaft_node.html

BCG. (2015). Boston consulting group perspectives: Global wealth 2015: Winning the growth game (T. B. Group, Hrsg.). https://www.bcgperspectives.com/content/articles/financial-institutions-growth-global-wealth-2015-winning-the-growth-game/?chapter=2

Biagosch. (2016). *Case study seminar – Kick off presentation – Merger purpose is dominantly, consolidating or complementary* (TU München, Hrsg.). München, Deutschland.

Bloomberg. (2015). www.bilanz.ch. Accessed June 16, 2016, from http://www.bilanz.ch/unternehmen/schweiz-erlegt-grossbanken-mehr-eigenmittel-auf-477451

Commerzbank. (2013). *Commerzank: Annual Report 2012 – The bank at your side*. (Commerzbank, Hrsg.). https://www.commerzbank.de/media/aktionaere/service/archive/konzern/2013_3/Geschaeftsbericht_2012_Konzern_EN.pdf

Commerzbank. (2015). *Commerzbank – eine Großbank mit über 140-jähriger Geschichte*. (Commerzbank, Hrsg.). https://www.commerzbank.de/media/konzern_1/geschichte/download_8/hist_CB-Geschichte_de.pdf

Commerzbank. (2016). *Commerzbank: Annual Report 2015 – Constantly improving*. (Commerzbank, Hrsg.). Accessed June 17, 2016, from https://www.commerzbank.com/media/en/aktionaere/haupt/2016_5/geschaeftsbericht_2015.pdf

Ernst&Young. (2015). Accessed June 17, 2016, from www.ey.com, http://www.ey.com/Publication/vwLUAssets/EY_Analyse_Top-Banken_USA_vs._Europa_-_September_2015/$FILE/EY%20Banken%20Europa%20vs%20%20USA%20Halbjahr%202%202015.pdf

European Commission. (2016). Accessed June 15, 2016, from http://ec.europa.eu/economy_finance/eu/forecasts/2016_winter_forecast_en.htm

Eurostat. (2015). Accessed September 15, 2016, from www.ec.europa.eu, http://ec.europa.eu/eurostat/tgm/table.do?tab=table&init=1&language=en&pcode=tec00115&plugin=1

Finma. (2014). *Eidgenössische Finanzmarktaufsich FINMA. The Swiss "too big to fail" regime*. www.finma.ch

riskarticles.com. (2011). Accessed June 18, 2016, from http://riskarticles.com/basel-iii-key-updates/

Schildbach, J. (2013). www.dbresearch.de, https://www.dbresearch.com/PROD/DBR_INTERNET_ENPROD/PROD0000000000320825.pdf

Statista 1. (2016). Accessed June 5, 2016, from http://de.statista.com/statistik/daten/studie/165637/umfrage/marktkapitalisierung-von-banken-in-europa/

Statista 2. (2016). Accessed June 15, 2016, from www.statista.de , http://www.statista.com/statistics/188165/annual-gdp-growth-of-the-united-states-since-1990/

Statista 3. (2016). Accessed June 2, 2016, from http://de.statista.com/statistik/daten/studie/165617/umfrage/bilanzsumme-von-banken-in-europa/

Strutz. (2008). *Commerzbank acquires Dresdner Bank* (Commerzbank, Hrsg.). https://www.commerzbank.com/media/aktionaere/vortrag_1/2008_4/080925_Unicredit_Konferenz.pdf

UBS. (2011). *UBS Investor Day*. (Z. a. UBS AG, Hrsg.) by Sergio Ermotti, Group Chief Executive Office. https://www.ubs.com/content/dam/static/global/investor_relations/UBS_2011_Investor-Day_CEO.pdf

UBS. (2012). *150 years of banking tradition*. (Z. a. UBS AG, Hrsg.). www.ubs.com, https://www.ubs.com/global/de/about_ubs/about_us/history.html

UBS. (2015). *UBS in ein paar Worten*. (Z. a. UBS AG, Hrsg.). www.ubs.com, https://www.ubs.com/global/de/about_ubs/about_us/ourprofile.html

UBS. (2016). *UBS Group AG and UBS AG Annual Report 2015*. (Z. a. UBS AG, Hrsg.). https://www.ubs.com/global/de/about_ubs/investor_relations/annualreporting/2015.html

Weber, A (2016). *Europe is over-banked* (CNBC, Interviewer). Accessed June 16, 2016, from http://www.cnbc.com/2016/04/18/ubs-axel-weber-europe-is-over-banked.html

weforum.org. (2015). Accessed June 17, 2016, from http://www3.weforum.org/docs/WEF_The_future__of_financial_services.pdf

worldretailbankingreport.com. (2016). Accessed June 18, 2016, from https://www.worldretailbankingreport.com/download

Recommended Readings

Adler, G., & Amann, W. (2011). *Case writing for executive education: A survival guide*. Charlotte, NC: Information Age Publishing.

Barnes, L., Christensen, C., & Hansen, A. (1994). *Teaching and the case method*. Boston, MA: Harvard Business School Press.

Campoy, R. (2005). *Case study analysis in the classroom*. Thousand Oaks, CA: Sage.

Ellet, W. (2007). *The case study handbook: How to read, discuss, and write persuasively about cases*. Boston, MA: Harvard Business School Press.

Espen, A., & Schiano, B. (2014). *Teaching with cases: A practical guide*. Boston, MA: Harvard Business School Publishing.

Garvin, D. (2007). Teaching executives and teaching MBAs: Reflections on the case method. *Academy of Management Learning & Education, 6*(3), 364–374.

Herreid, C., Herreid, K., & Schiller, N. (2012). *Science stories – Using case studies to teach critical thinking*. Arlington, VA: National Science Teachers Association.

Hersum, A., & McNair, M. (1967). *The case method at the Harvard Business School*. New York: McGraw-Hill.

Jonassen, D. (2011). *Learning to solve problems*. New York: Routledge.

Kaye, R., & Hawkridge, D. (Eds.). (2003). *Learning and teaching for business, case studies of successful innovation*. London: Kogan Page.

Lynn, L. (1999). *Teaching and learning with cases*. New York: Chatham House Publishers.

Naumes, W., & Naumes, M. J. (1999). *The art & craft of case writing*. Thousand Oaks, CA: Sage.

Piekkari, R., & Welch, C. (Eds.). (2010). *Rethinking the case study in international business research*. Northampton, MA: Edward Elgar.

Vega, G. (2017). *The case writing workbook*. Florence: Taylor and Francis.

Winterburn, R. (1987). *Case study method in management development*. London: Commonwealth Secretariat.

Yin, R. (2014). *Case study research*. London: Sage.

G. Friedl, A. Biagosch (eds.), *Case Studies in Strategic Management*, Management for Professionals, https://doi.org/10.1007/978-3-319-95555-1

MIX
Papier aus verantwortungsvollen Quellen
Paper from responsible sources
FSC® C105338

If you have any concerns about our products,
you can contact us on
ProductSafety@springernature.com

In case Publisher is established outside the EU,
the EU authorized representative is:
Springer Nature Customer Service Center GmbH
Europaplatz 3, 69115 Heidelberg, Germany

Printed by Libri Plureos GmbH
in Hamburg, Germany